SUSAN ALDWORTH

You are lying on a bed looking up at your brain scan live on a bank of monitors. You are seeing the inside of your brain with your brain. You are thinking about what you are seeing with what you are seeing on the screen. You are looking inside your head while thinking, seeing, feeling – your brain is working while you are looking inside it. But where is the 'me' in all this?

Susan Aldworth, Christmas Day 1999

SUSAN ALDWORTH'S ART explores the nature of consciousness. In 1999, the experience of observing her brain live on a monitor during a diagnostic brain scan triggered an ongoing fascination with the relationship between the physical brain and the sense of self. Since then Aldworth has worked and collaborated with doctors, neuroscientists, neuropsychologists, etchers, artists and musicians in pursuit of this elusive subject. She has observed numerous brain scans in hospitals and undergone research brain scans herself to try and make sense of the material basis of personality. In parallel with these investigations she has experimented with etching techniques in collaboration with master etcher Nigel Oxley, and developed a radical method whose chemical processes are analogous to those in the brain that might be responsible for personality. Aldworth also works with animated film, digital print and light installation. *Scribing the Soul* is the result of her tracking consciousness over the past seven years.

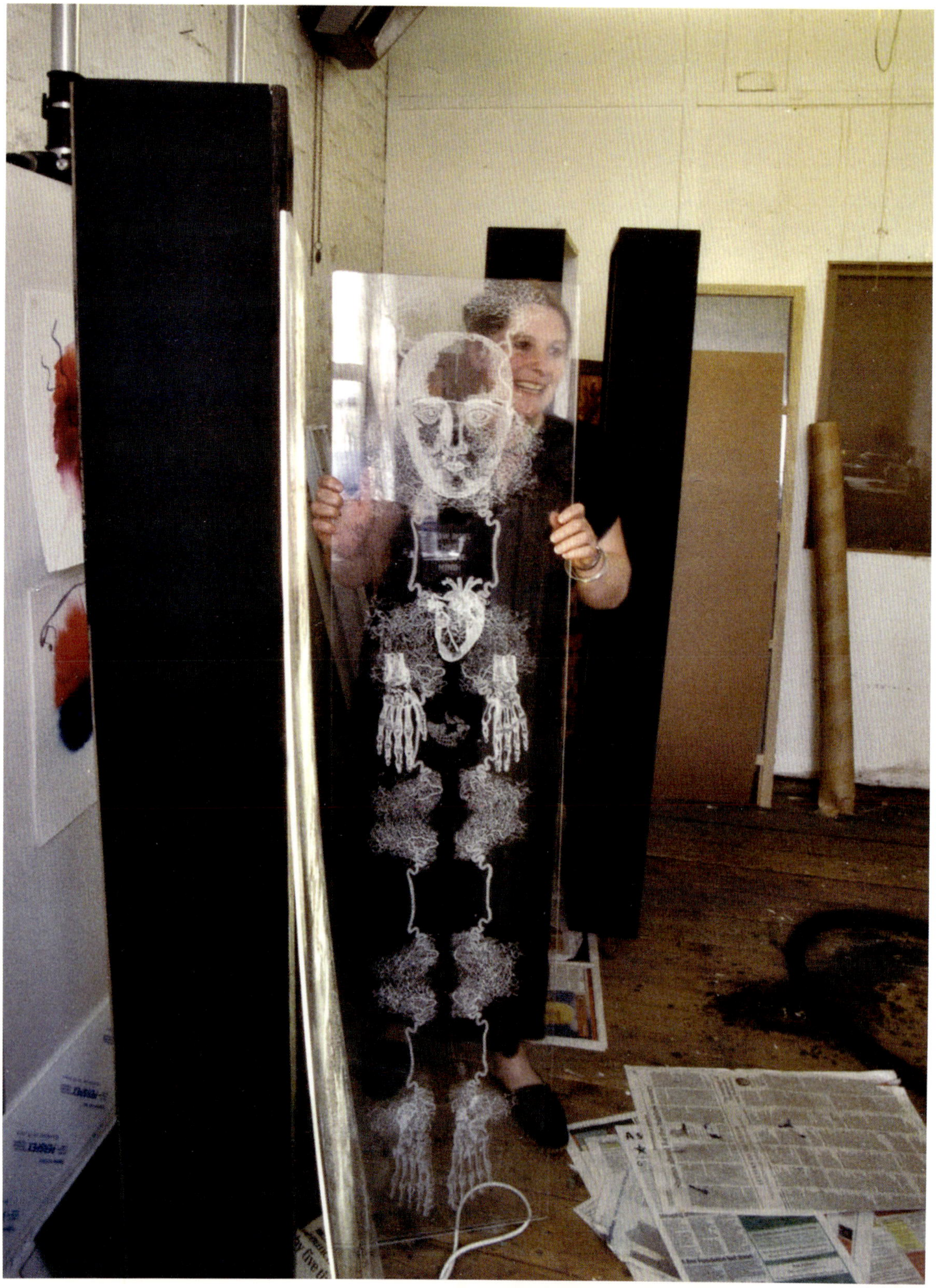

RESIDENCIES AND APPOINTMENTS

2007 Research Fellow, London Metropolitan University
Invited Artist, Cuenca Biennial, Ecuador
Curator, *Arts and Minds*, Westminster Arts
Artist collaboration, Institute of Neuroscience, University of Newcastle
Arts Council Touring Grant, *Scribing the Soul*
Wellcome Trust Arts Award, *This Fatal Subject*

2006 Director, London Arts and Health Forum
Curator, *The Thames*, ING Bank
Artist in Residence, Gordon Museum of Pathology, King's College London

2005 Artist in Residence, Royal London Hospital
Artist in Residence, London Metropolitan University
Director, Transition Gallery, London

2004 Curator, East Wing Collection of Outsider Art, Homerton Hospital

2003 Artist in Residence, East Wing, Homerton Hospital, London

ONE-PERSON SHOWS

2007 *Matter into Imagination*, Medical Museum, Cuenca, Ecuador

2006 *Matter into Imagination*, Menier Gallery; Royal London Hospital;
Old Operating Theatre Museum, London

2004 *No Ghost in the Machine* installation, Cheltenham Science Festival

2002 *Between a Thing and a Thought*, Whitechapel Gallery;
Royal London Hospital
Gilding the Lily, V&A (Friends' Room), London

1999 *L'esprit de l'escalier*, V&A (Friends' Room), London

SELECTED GROUP EXHIBITIONS

2007 Halloween Short Film Festival, ICA, London
Mapping the Imagination, V&A, London

2006 East End Film Festival, London
SuperShorts Film Festival, London
Video Exhibition, Primo Piano Living Gallery, Lecce, Italy

2005 New Art, Birmingham

2004 *Brave New World*, ING Bank, London

2002 *Brain Up*, Palais des Congrès, Paris
Drawing for All 2002, Gainsborough House, Sudbury

CONTRIBUTORS

PAUL BROKS is a neuropsychologist based at Plymouth University. Having for many years combined clinical practice and scientific research he has lately developed a profile as a writer. His book *Into the Silent Land* mixes neurological case stories, fiction and memoir. It was short-listed for the *Guardian* First Book Award and inspired a play, *On Ego* (co-written with Mick Gordon), which was performed to wide acclaim at the Soho Theatre. Among other recent projects, Broks has collaborated with the filmmaker Ian Knox to write and present a documentary feature film, *Martino Unstrung*, which tells the story of the brain-damaged jazz guitar virtuoso, Pat Martino (Sixteen Films, 2008). A second book, *The Laws of Magic* (Atlantic Books), is forthcoming.

ROBERT MASON is a freelance artist and writer, who has contributed to *Blueprint, Eye, Varoom, Étapes Graphiques* and other publications. He graduated from the Royal College of Art in 1976 and is currently a lecturer at Norwich School of Art & Design, having previously worked at Chelsea, St Martin's, Leeds and many other institutions. He has illustrated extensively, nationally and internationally. His previous publications include *A Digital Dolly?* and *Mere Illustration*, and he is now completing a satirical novel about British Art Schools. He lives in Norwich, but if the novel – *Ant Farm* – is ever published, he will be forced to emigrate and assume a new identity.

GILL SAUNDERS joined the V&A in 1979. She is now Senior Curator (Prints) in the Word & Image Department of the Victoria & Albert Museum. She has curated a number of V&A exhibitions, most recently *Mapping the Imagination* (3 October 2007 – 27 April 2008), and her publications include *The Nude: A New Perspective* (1989), *Recording Britain* (1990), *Picturing Plants: An Analytical History of Botanical Illustration* (1995) and *Wallpaper in Interior Decoration* (2002). She was a major contributor to *Impressions of the 20th Century*, ed. M. Timmers (2001). Her most recent books are *Prints Now: Directions and Definitions* (2006), co-authored with Rosie Miles, and *Sian Bowen: Gaze* (2007).

In 1997–98 she was the V&A Exchange Fellow at Sussex University, teaching courses on 20th century and contemporary art. She continues to teach at the V&A and elsewhere, and lectures and broadcasts regularly.

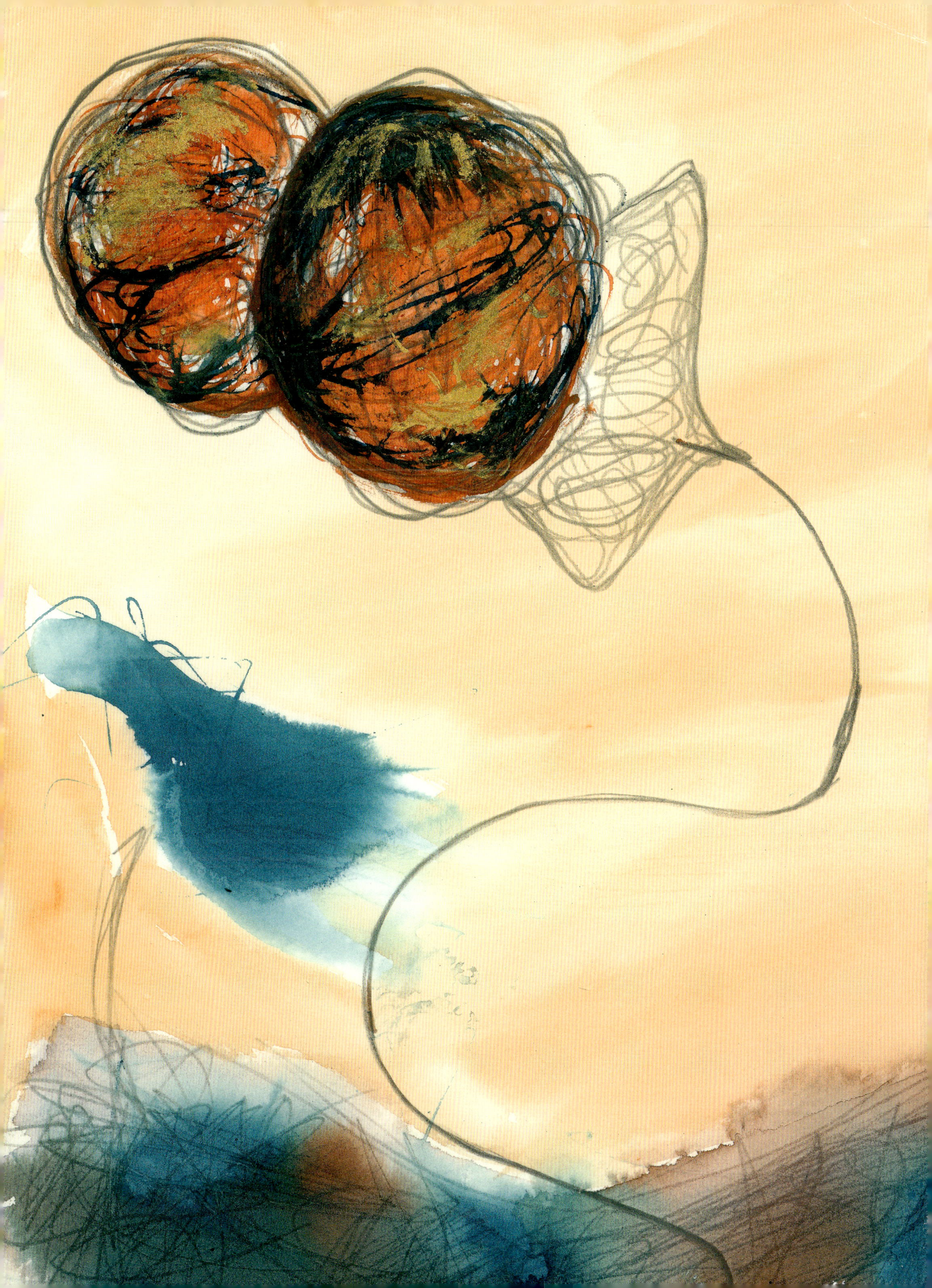

6

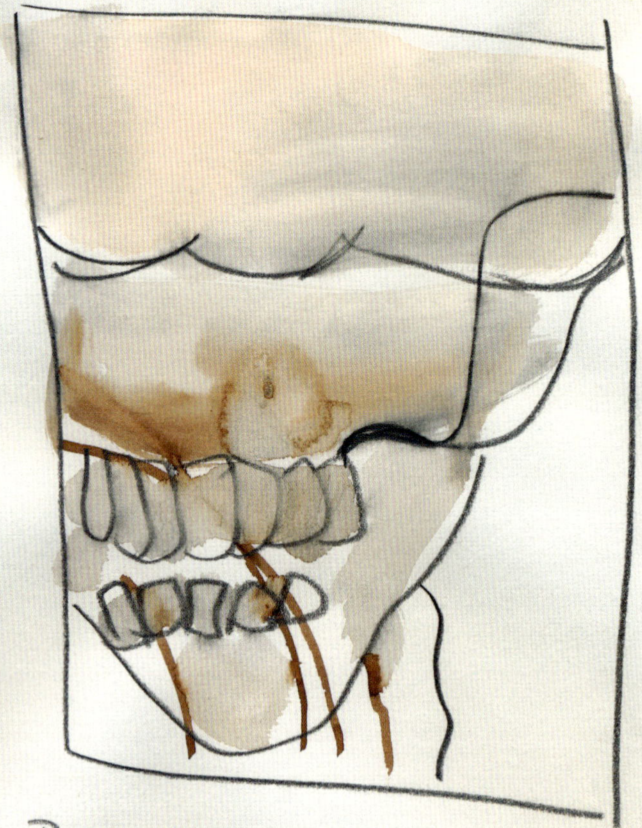

Beginning – ringing bell.

SCRIBING THE SOUL

SUSAN ALDWORTH

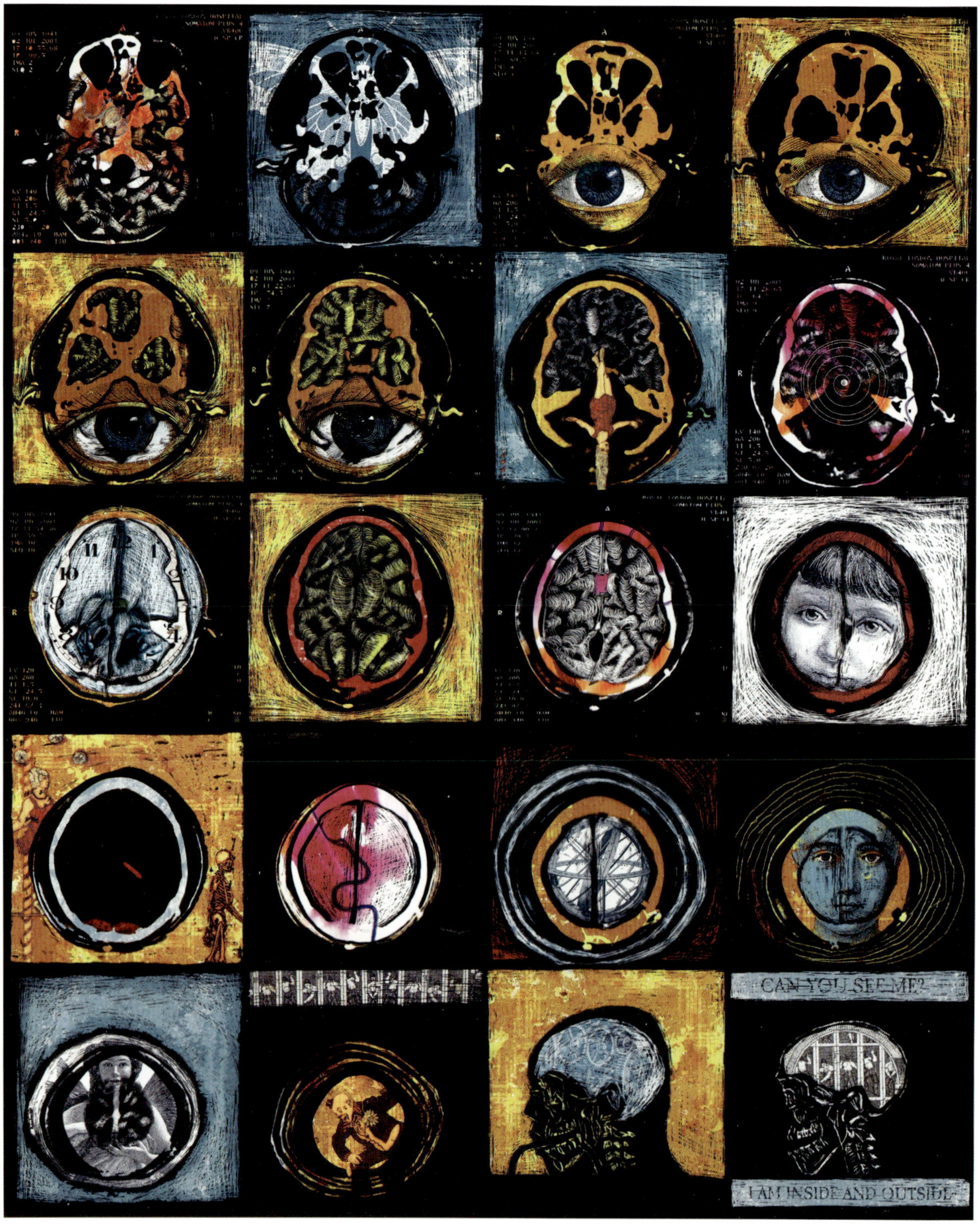
CAN YOU SEE ME?
I AM INSIDE AND OUTSIDE

CONTENTS

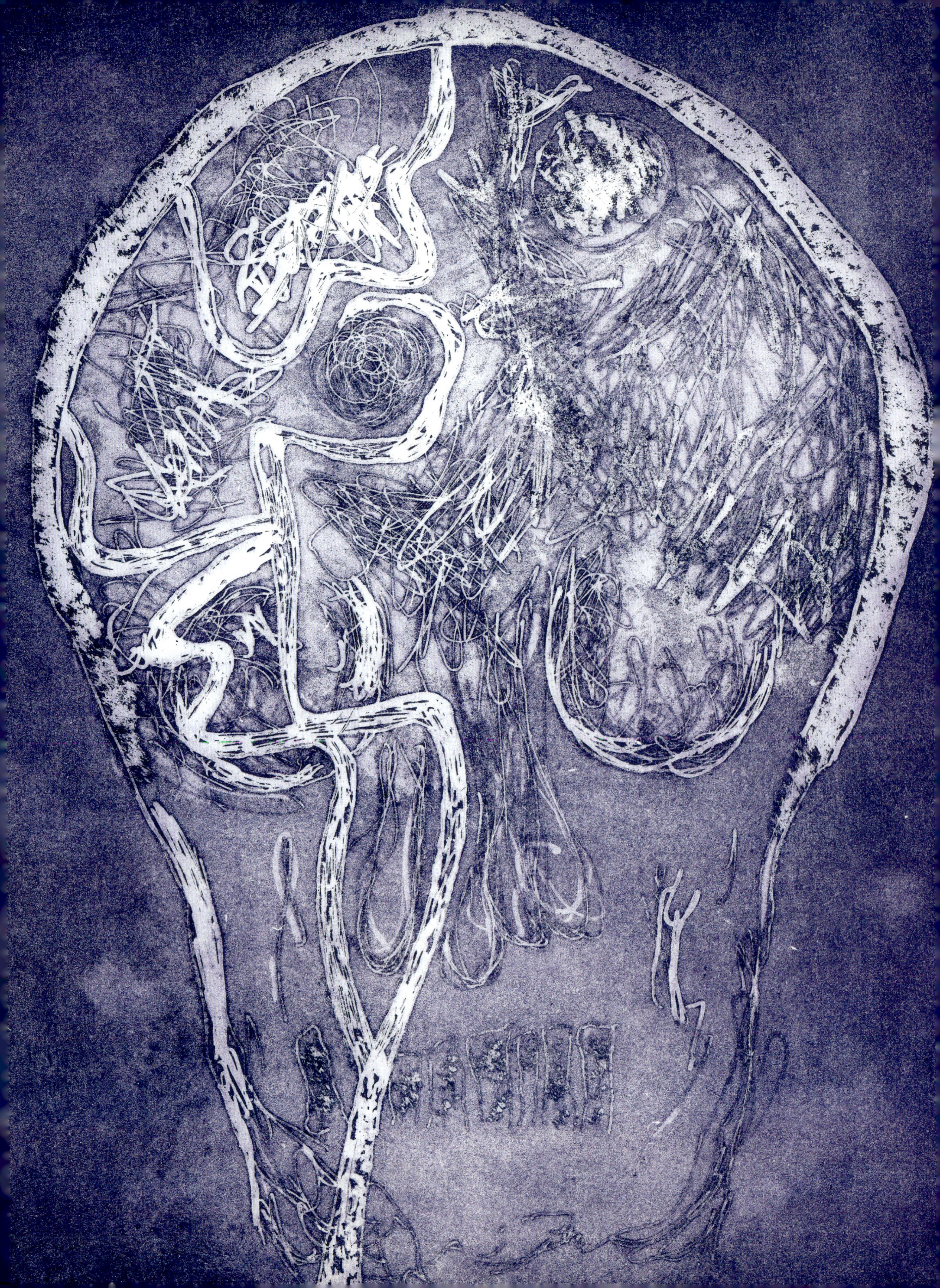

GILL SAUNDERS

STATES OF MIND

Noosphere ... the living membrane which is stretched like a film over the lustrous surface of the star which holds us. An ultimate envelope taking on its own individuality and gradually detaching itself like a luminous aura.

Pierre Teilhard de Chardin, The Phenomenon of Man, *1955*[1]

TEILHARD DE CHARDIN, Jesuit priest and palaeontologist, synthesized his faith in God and his faith in science to envision an evolving Creation in which the noosphere (the sphere of human thought, from the Greek 'nous', meaning mind) was the third in a succession of phases of the development of the Earth. First came the geosphere (inanimate matter); then the biosphere (biological life); and then, with the emergence of human cognition, the noosphere. Chardin postulated the idea that this net of human consciousness enveloped the globe, and comprised 'myriad grains of thought' or 'individual reflections' grouped into a collective mind or what we might call a collective consciousness.[2]

Susan Aldworth's extraordinary prints, inspired by scans of the brains of patients at the Neuroradiology department of the Royal London Hospital, might be read as vivid illustrations of Chardin's theory. Comprising constellations of nerves and neural networks, luminous webs of connective tissues, each image shows an 'organism of Mind' or, in Aldworth's own words (echoing Chardin), an instance of the 'birth of thought'. Each of her 'Brainscapes' (the series title for a sequence of etchings made in 2005–6) might be taken to represent one of these 'grains of thought' which together cohere in an encompassing human consciousness, a 'portrait' of what it is to be human. I am reminded of Helen Chadwick's 1991 *Self-Portrait*[3] in which the artist is seen cradling a brain in her hands, a fragile treasure swathed in folds of silken cloth like a holy relic; presented without reference to gender, age or race, it becomes a collective self-portrait of mankind, in which consciousness – this ability to contemplate one's own mind – is synonymous with human identity. Likewise Aldworth's etchings, in one sense peculiarly intimate 'portraits' in that they record or represent the brain scans of individuals, have been transmuted from specific to generic, from personal to universal.

Brainscape 5 2006 etching and aquatint 30 x 25 cms

THOUGH THEY ADDRESS an aspect of anatomy using the tools of medical imaging, investigation and treatment, these prints are not medical illustrations in the conventional sense; they are visual equivalents for the brain's activity, representing the electrical charges, the chemical reactions which constitute thought, consciousness, and neurological event. In them organic forms bloom and spark in the deep space of blue (the *Brainscapes*) or black (*Birth of Thought* series) grounds. Are these meditations on beauty, the expressions of emotion (love, fear), or the manifestations of trauma in the brain – a haemorrhage, a seizure, the aftermath of a stroke? Their ambiguity reinforces our sense that the mind – and the phenomenon of consciousness – remains an unfathomable mystery. A dissection of the brain or a colour-coded scan can elucidate the physical aspects, and allow us to grasp the structure, the circuitry, but the process – and the very concept of consciousness and thought – remains elusive, something we can understand only obliquely through the medium of metaphor and analogy. Aldworth's etchings compound this mystery even as they illuminate it.

ALDWORTH HAS MADE several series of etchings, as well as digital prints, drawings and films, all addressing this subject – part of an ongoing exploration which has consumed her since her own experience of undergoing a cerebral angiogram seven years ago. Aldworth is not alone in applying the revelatory technologies of diagnostic imaging in the pursuit of understanding identity, in seeking the site of our sense of self-hood, nor is she the only artist employing the visual language of medicine in the making of portraits. When Mona Hatoum recorded a visceral voyage through her own body, by means of video endoscopy, she offered a peculiarly intimate self-portrait, an interior landscape of pulsing flesh, but she gave it the title *Corps étranger* ('Foreign Body').[4] When asked about this apparent contradiction she explained 'we don't have access to our insides except [...] when we go to hospital and discover we have a terrible disease, so [...] the internal workings of our body are completely foreign to us most of the time.'[5] This of course is the conundrum that intrigues Aldworth, and has provoked her various attempts to make this foreign landscape of the brain – of the mind itself – visible and accessible to us. A number of her prints, especially the *Brainscapes* and the *Birth of a Thought* sequence (2006–7), read like maps of the brain's activity described through its neural pathways, the network of

Birth of a Thought 3, 4 2007 etching and aquatint, each 50 x 65 cms

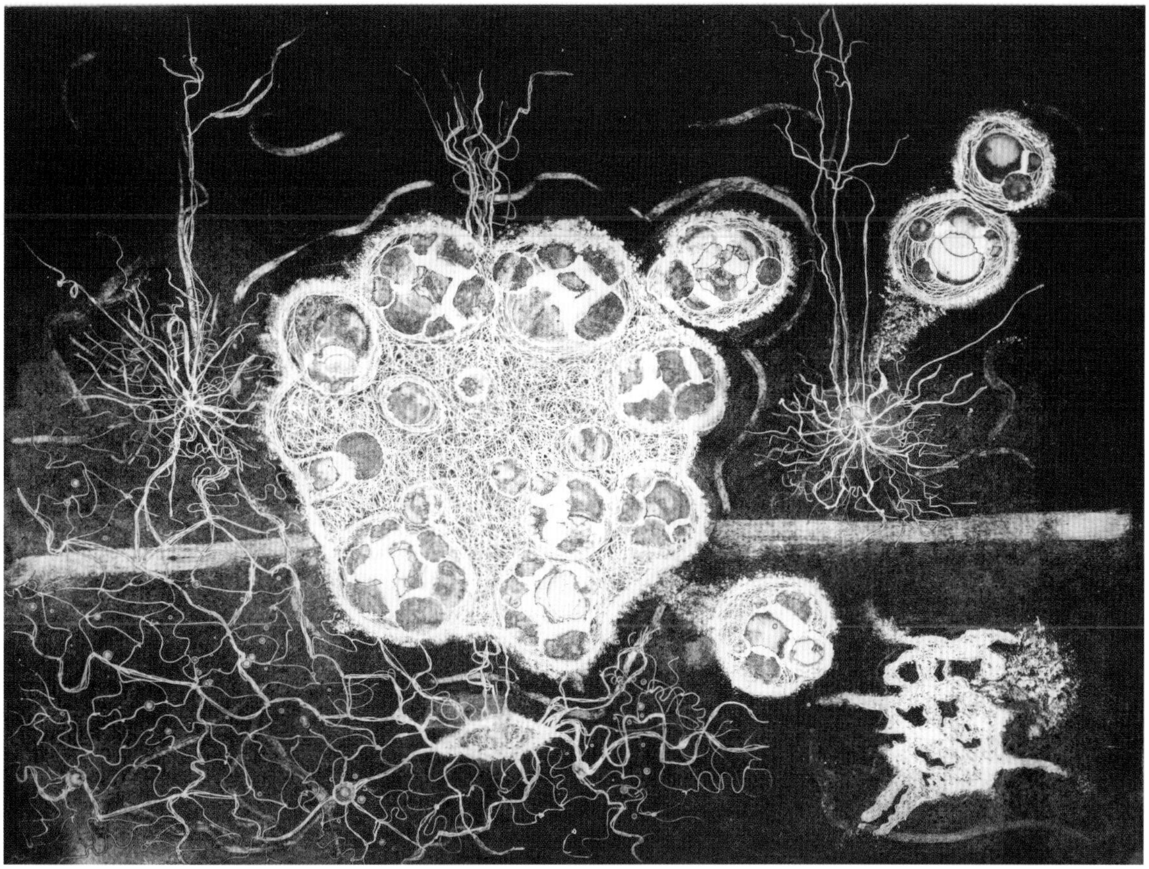

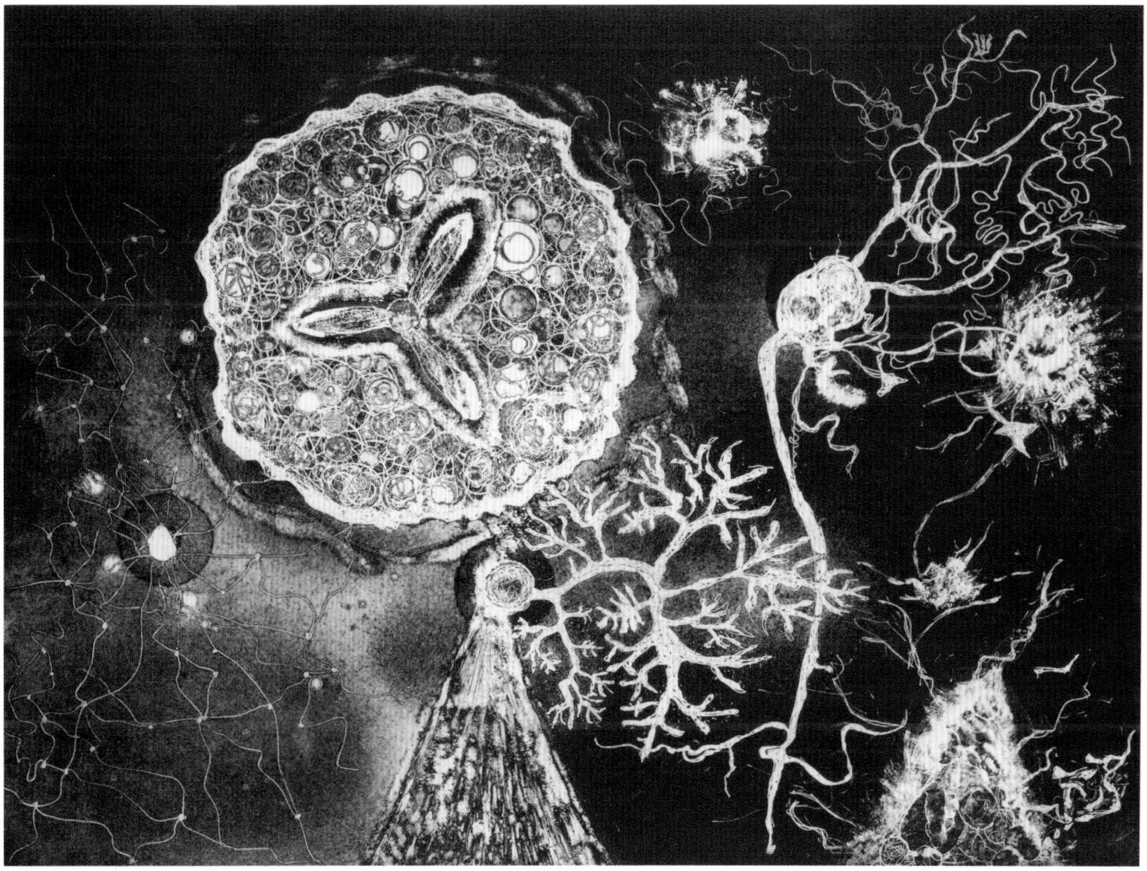

nerves, blood vessels and cells. As illustrations of its convoluted topography these are guides to uncharted territory. But always the emphasis is on this fundamental struggle to describe and understand – to 'grasp' – the essence of consciousness. This is vividly dramatised in the series *The Self is a Shadow Puppet* (2007; also etchings) in which hands (each opened wide in a gesture of wonder) reach up and out of the darkness towards a disembodied image of the brain framed by shimmering cilia-like forms.

ALDWORTH'S ETCHINGS DERIVE from or are inspired by her drawings of the same subjects but they are by no means direct reproductions of these drawings, nor are they intended to be; the drawings and watercolours are independent works, but they are also the starting point from which the prints expand by an innovative exploitation of the nature and characteristic qualities of printmaking to create images which are the graphic equivalents of the processes they describe.

Of course printmaking has always been a medium of experiment, invention, accident and alchemy, with its progress through successive states, the productions of proofs, the corrections, calculations and serendipitous discoveries, the uncertainties inherent in the use of acids and inks. Aldworth has worked with fellow artist and master printmaker Nigel Oxley, and together they have collaborated to push the boundaries of the etching process, developing what they describe as 'a radical form of "white line" etching which uses chemical reactions on the surface of the plate to mirror chemical activity in the brain.'[6] In the *Brainscapes* and the *Birth of a Thought* series Aldworth has discovered the perfect marriage of medium and subject, choosing to interpret the medical data through the potential offered by etching. Of all the printmaking techniques, etching is perhaps the best suited to her aims and the expression of her ideas. Oxley has acknowledged this, commenting 'you let the process find its own life'.[7] Indeed it is this capacity afforded by etching, this potential to generate imagery in and of itself, which is directly analogous to the neurological events Aldworth observed in the scans. The etchings are records of their own making which mirror the mind at work.

It was Oxley's experience and technical expertise which enabled Aldworth to work on an unusually large scale (the most recent etchings are 'huge…at the limit of the aquatint box!'[8]) but also to push the process

Shadow Puppet 7 2007 etching and aquatint 50 x 35 cms

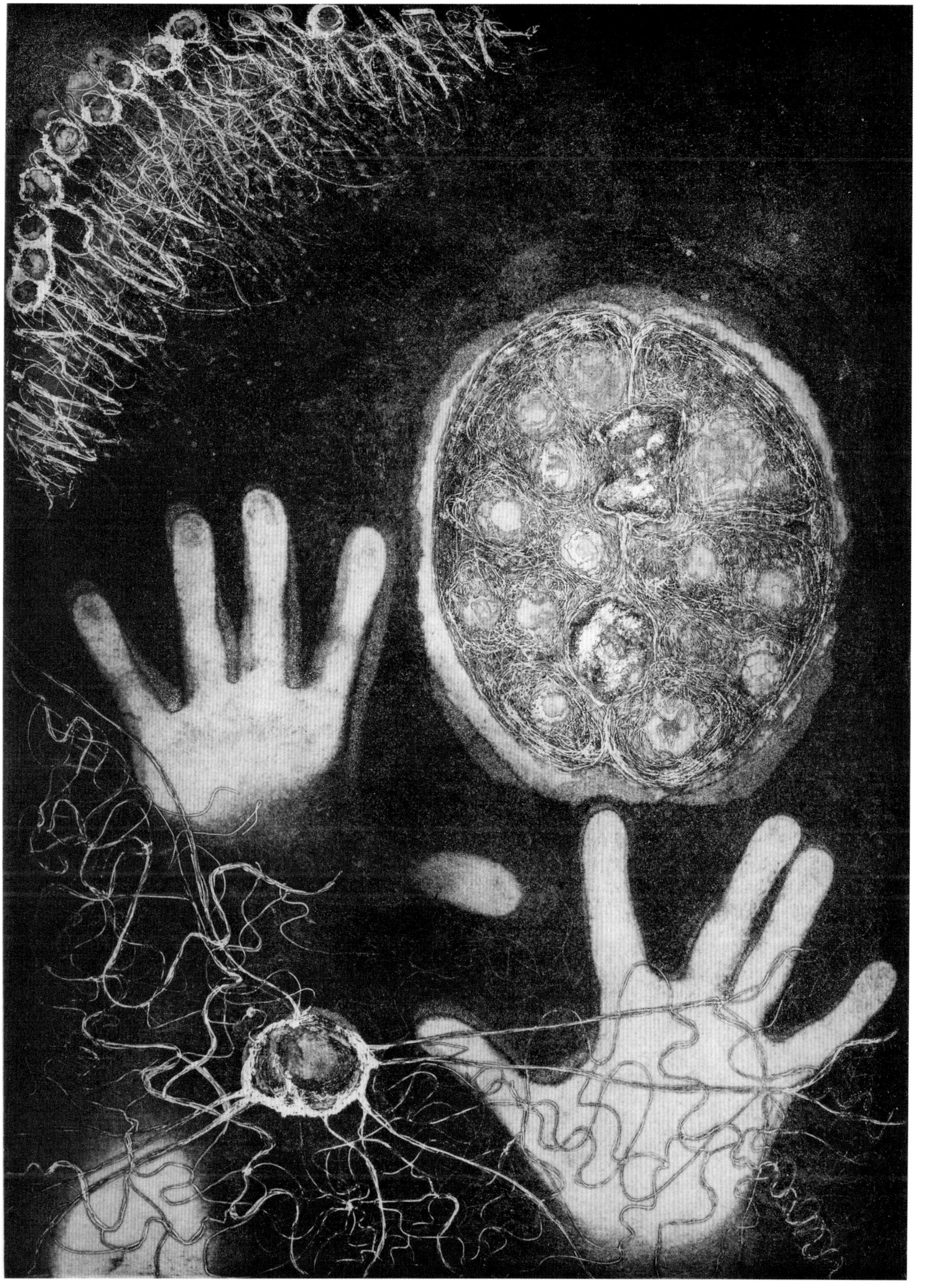

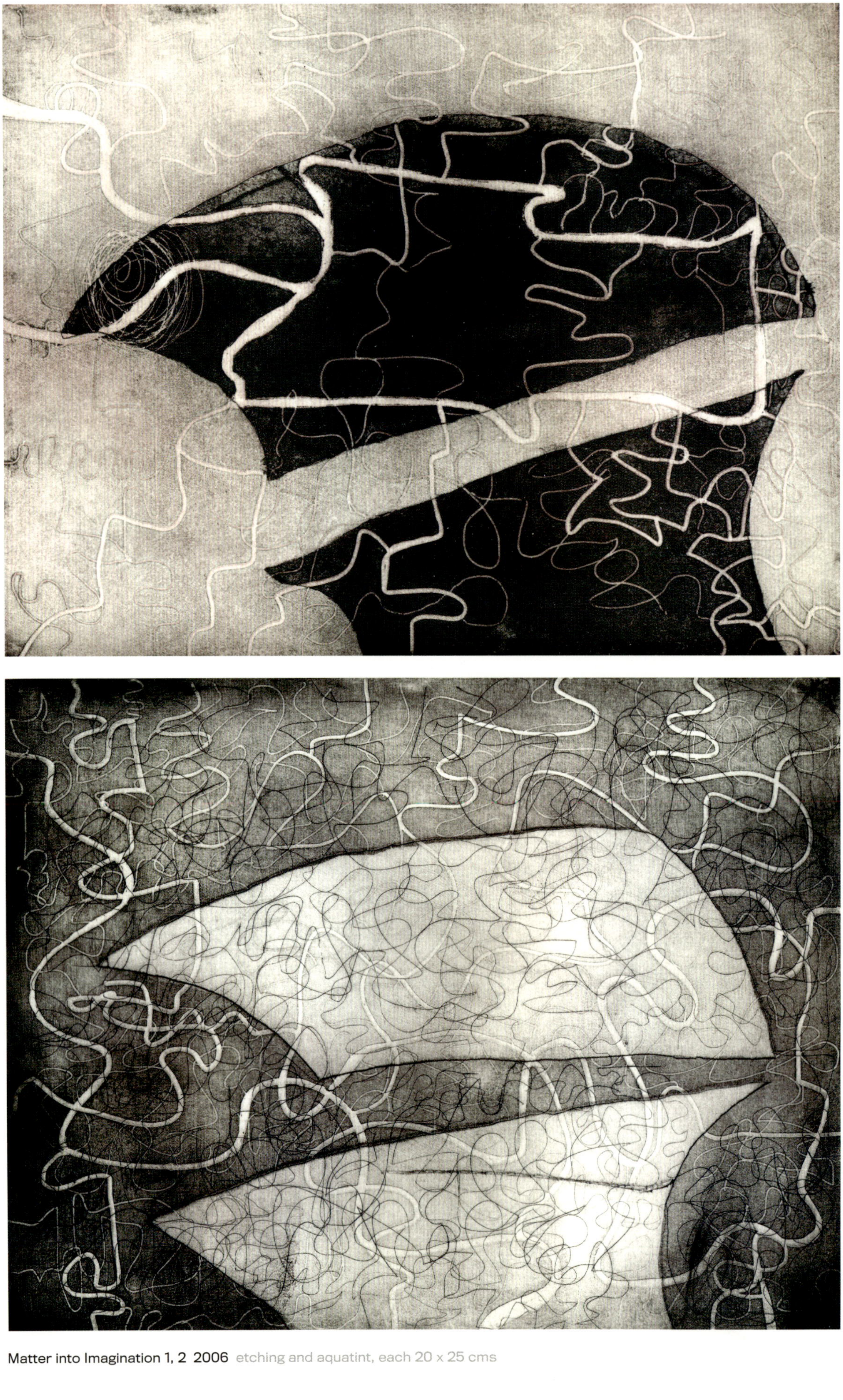

Matter into Imagination 1, 2 2006 etching and aquatint, each 20 x 25 cms

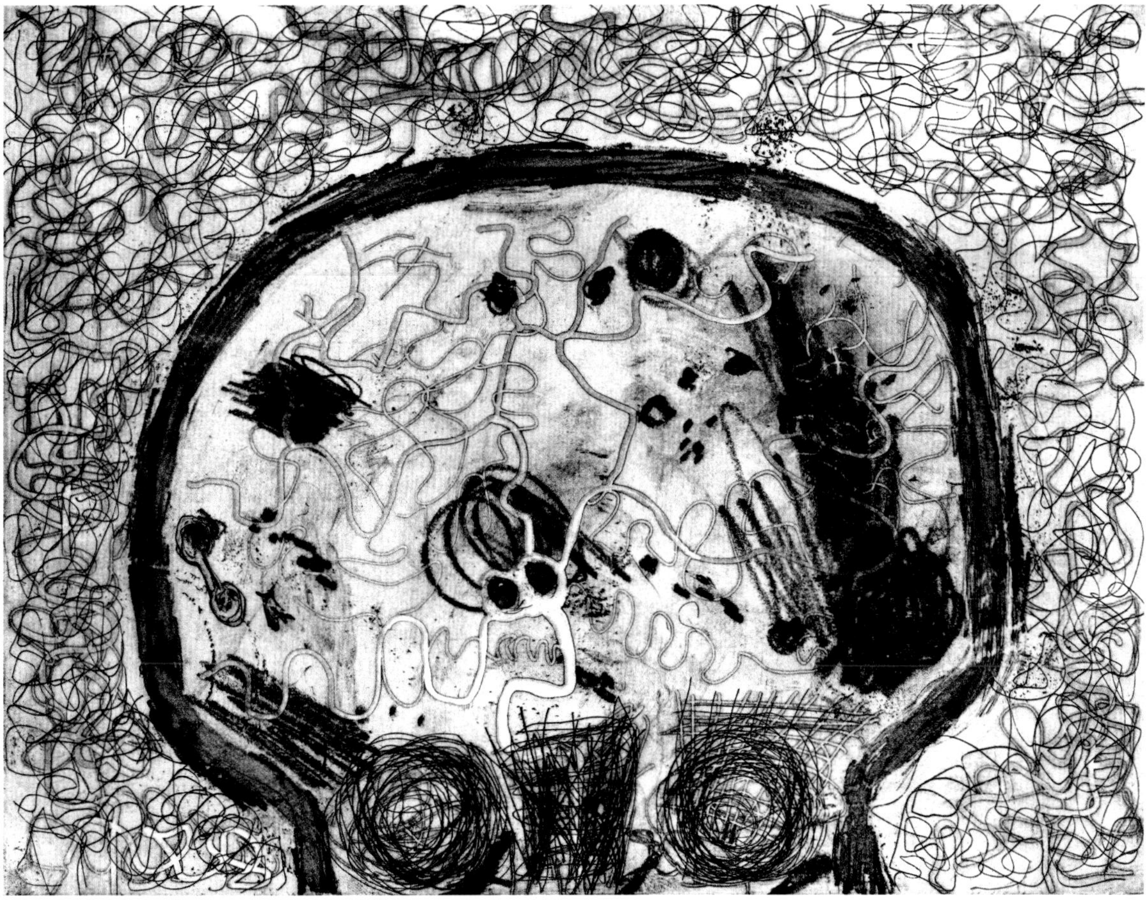

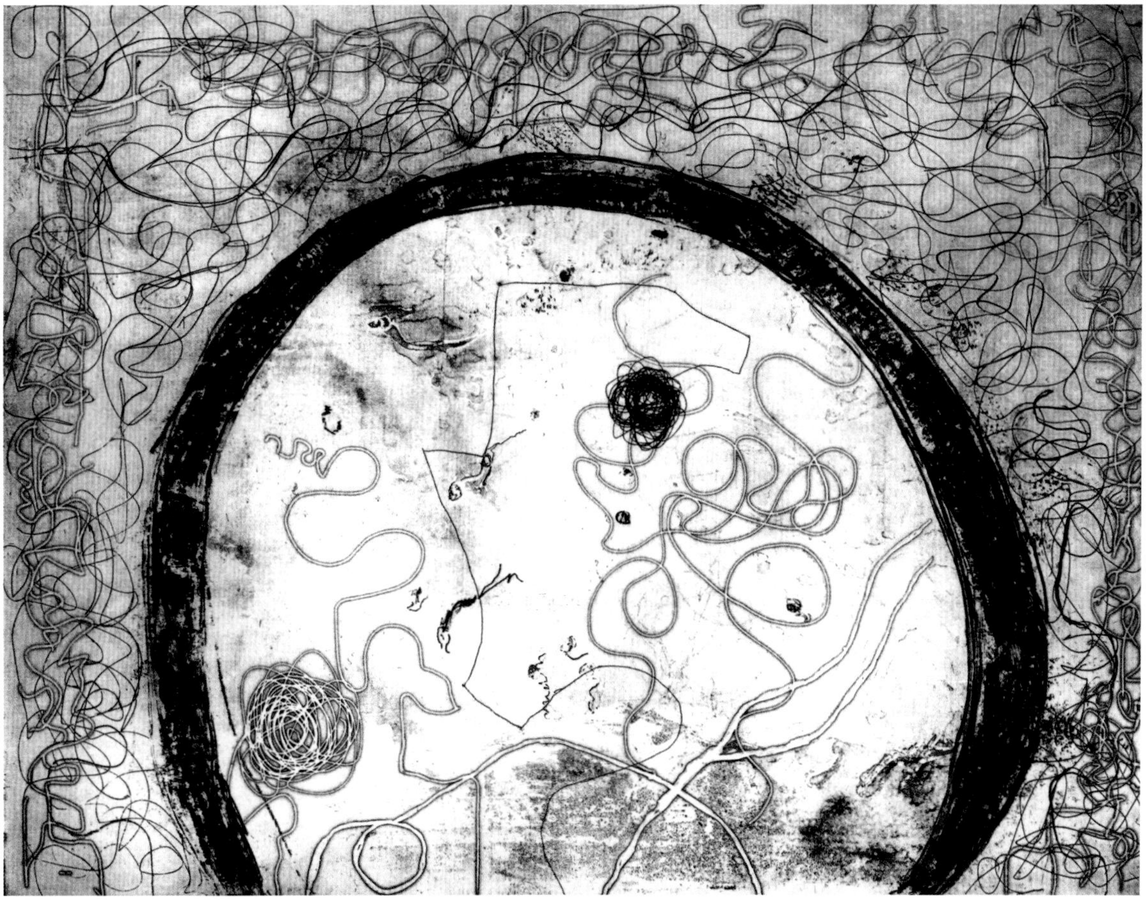

Thought Process 2005 top Birth of a Thought 1 2005 etching and aquatint, each 20 x 25 cms

in new directions, 'taking bits of old vocabulary and turning them into something else.'[9] In their experiments with negative, or 'white line', etching they discovered by chance that a line drawn on the etching plate using a permanent marker acted as a resist. This gave an unprecedented fluency to the etchings, but also offered a graphic equivalent for the negative line seen in cerebral angiograms. This method of working entirely with white line, producing a strong contrast with the rich aquatint grounds, was especially important to Aldworth: the white lines introduce an emphatic light which she sees as suggestive of the personality of the patients, and a means of expressing their individual consciousness. Aldworth and Oxley also allowed the unpredictable effects of their materials to produce serendipitous effects – as when they let methylated spirits bleed into white spirit, resulting in a fluid organic imagery that mimics the chemical reactions in the brain itself.

THE BRAINSCAPE ETCHINGS are printed in a rich evocative blue pigment. Aldworth describes the appearance of this colour in her work almost as if it were an independent phenomenon generated by the work itself: 'An intense blue was beginning to emerge in my studio work – which I later call[ed] cerebral blue. It is a colour which many patients say they associate with brain trauma.'[10] The echoes and associations of this blue reach beyond the particular circumstances of artist and subject in ways which resonate with the wider meaning and context; painter Sam Francis claimed it as 'the colour of speculation',[11] and again there are analogies between Aldworth's work and that of Helen Chadwick. The central feature of Chadwick's magnificent installation *The Oval Court* (1986)[12] is a collage of photocopies printed in a deep blue. She described her choice thus: 'it seemed to me that the colour where one cannot determine gravity or perspective is blue'.[13] Marina Warner, writing of Chadwick's work, reminds us that blue is the colour of the mysterious and the unknown, as we acknowledge in the phrase 'out of the blue';[14] indeed it can also refer to something unexpected – apt in relation to Aldworth's use of blue since brain traumas such as aneurysms often strike without warning. These ideas are expanded by the philosopher William Gass in his essay *On Being Blue*, where he says that 'colour is consciousness itself, colour is feeling ... Of the colours blue and green have the greatest emotional range ... Blue is therefore the most suitable as the colour of interior life.'[15]

Brainscape 24 2006 etching and aquatint 30 x 25 cms

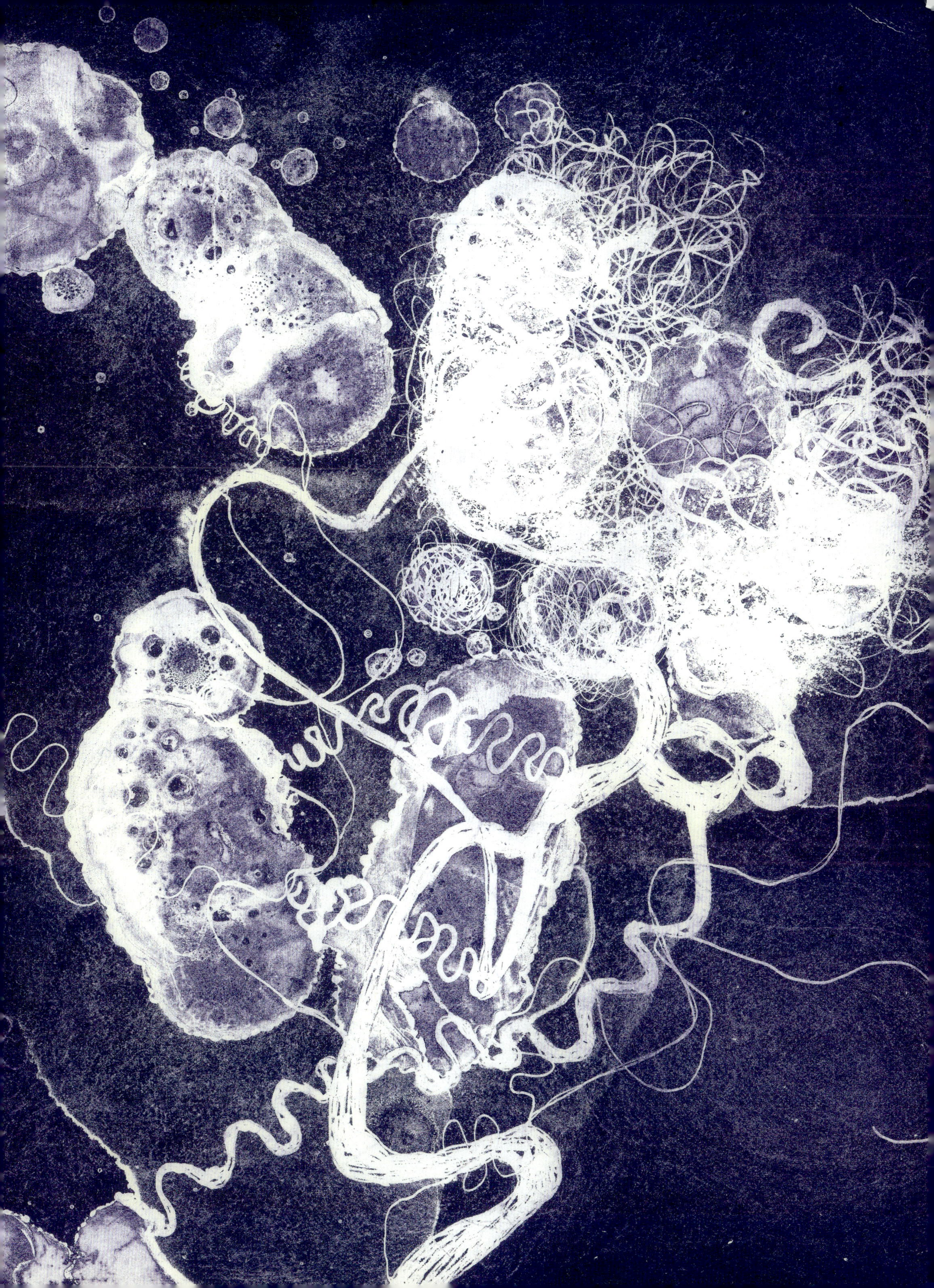

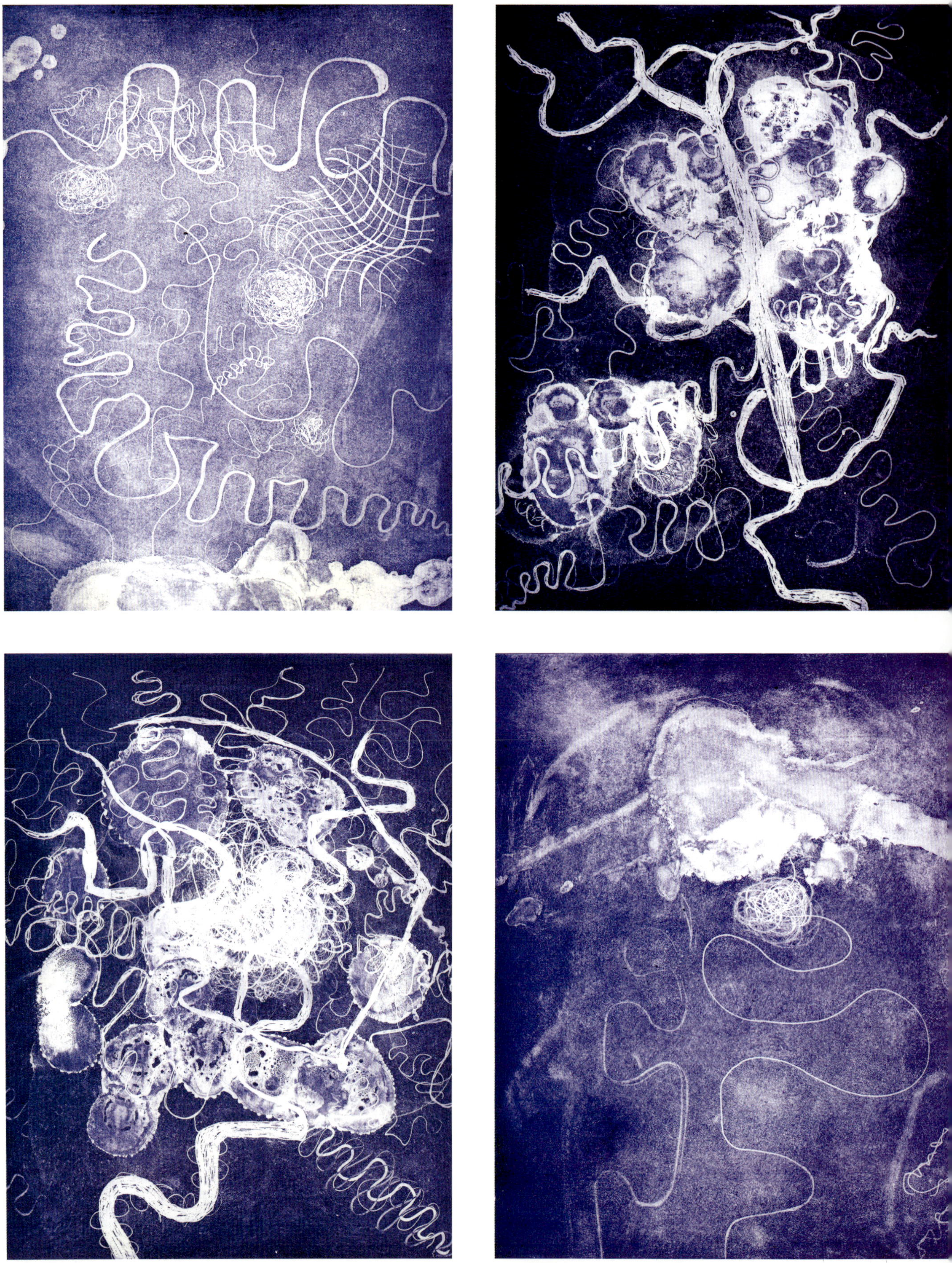

Brainscape series 8, 18, 1, 21 top 28, 7, 22, 23 2006 etching and aquatint, each 30 x 25 cms

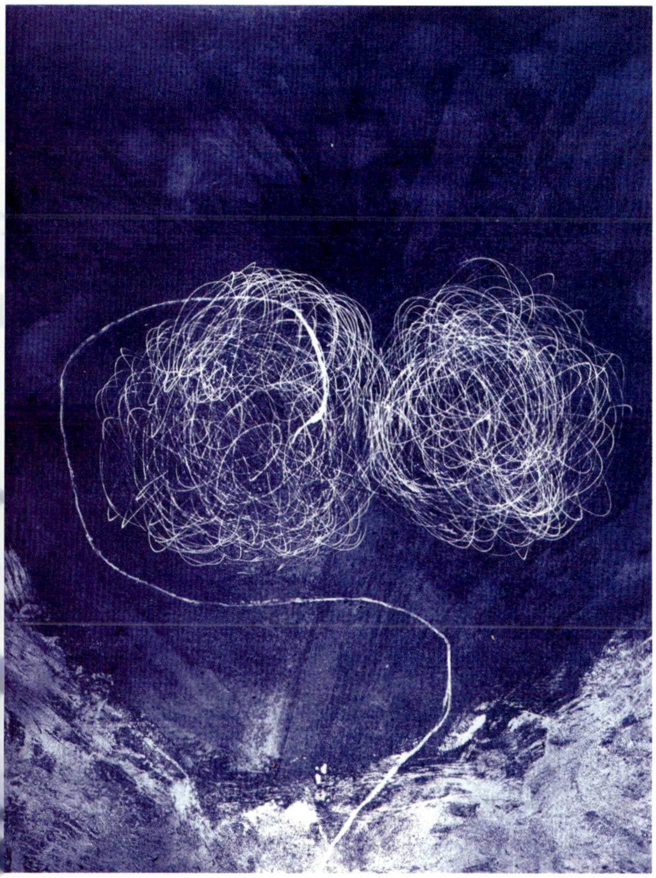

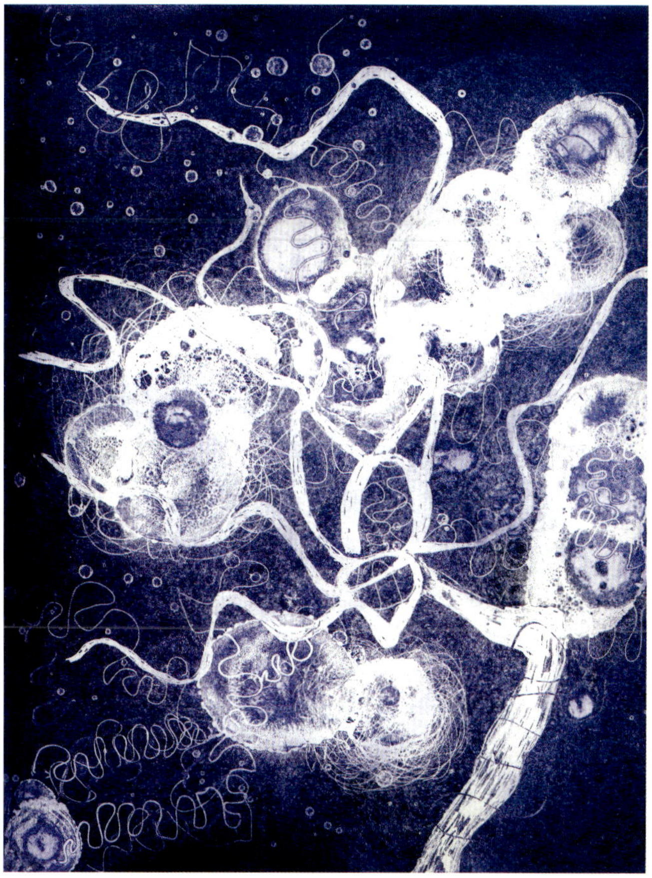

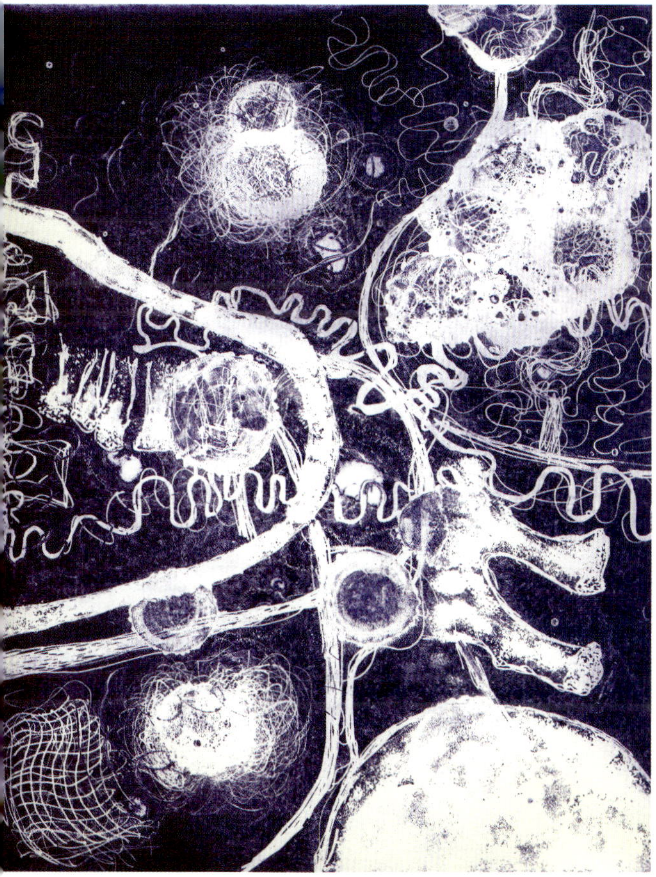

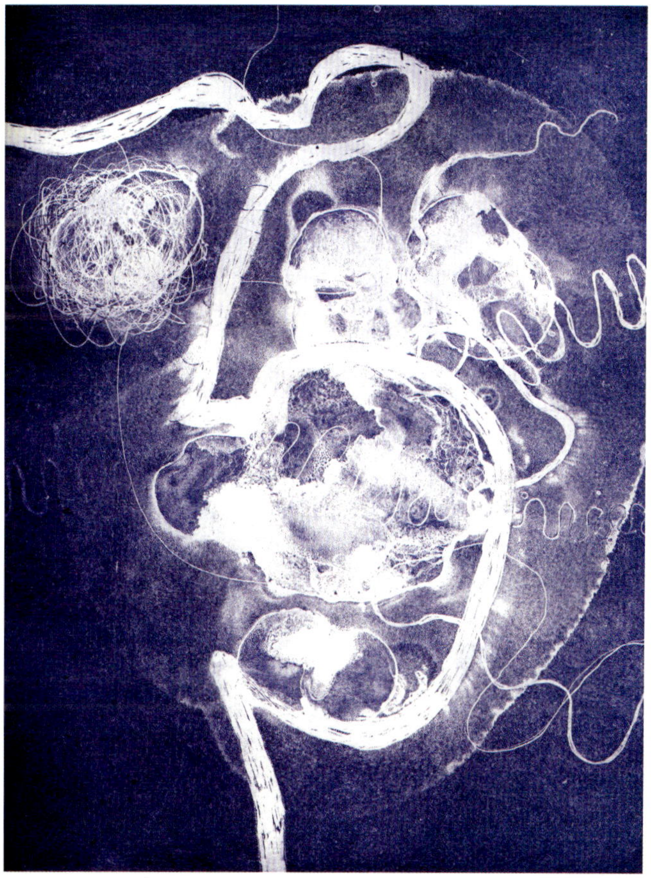

Colour of mind, spirit, and transcendence, this rich blue which Aldworth favours also has a specific scientific association: it is strongly reminiscent of the cyanotype (or blueprint) process. Cyanotype, an early photographic process invented by Sir John Herschel in 1842, was used almost exclusively for making photograms or 'photogenic drawings'. Amongst the earliest and best known applications of the process are the botanical illustrations of Anna Atkins (1799–1871), who made exquisite records of ephemeral organic materials such as algae, seaweeds and wild flowers, which were effectively unique self-portraits of the specimens. This blue is thus indelibly associated with a spirit of scientific enquiry and experiment, allied with aesthetic effect, and belongs to the history of recording fragile and fugitive phenomena.

Bringing together the subjective with the objective, Aldworth's prints belong to a distinguished tradition in which art is the partner to science in the advance of insight and understanding of the human condition. Through the medium of etching – a process crucially dependent on chemical reactions – she has produced prints which embody the act of the creation, and in the process she gives us extraordinarily intimate portraits of the mind in action. In these prints we see the luminous aura of Chardin's noosphere incarnated in images of our 'thinking flesh'.[16]

1 All quotes from Teilhard de Chardin are taken from *The Phenomenon of Man* (Harper & Row: New York, 1975).
2 I am grateful to Christopher Bucklow for an enlightening conversation on Teilhard de Chardin's theories.
3 Collection of National Galleries of Scotland.
4 *Corps étranger*, 1994. Video installation. Collection of Centre Georges Pompidou, Paris.
5 Mona Hatoum in an interview with John Tusa, 4 September 2005 (BBC Radio 3).
6 Susan Aldworth, 'The physical brain and the sense of self: an artist's exploration' (lecture, 2007; unpublished).
7 'Collective thinking' [Nigel Oxley in conversation with Susan Aldworth], *Printmaking Today*, Vol. 15, No. 2, summer 2006, p. 27.
8 In an email from the artist to this author, 12 March 2007.
9 *Printmaking Today*. See note 7.
10 Susan Aldworth lecture. See note 6.
11 Sam Francis, *Saturated Blue: Writings from the Notebooks* (Santa Monica: The Lapis Press, 1995).
12 Collection of the Victoria & Albert Museum.
13 Quoted in *Of Mutability: Helen Chadwick* (ICA: London, 1986), n.p.
14 Marina Warner, 'In the Garden of Earthly Delights: Helen Chadwick's "Of Mutability"', in *Of Mutability: Helen Chadwick*. See note 13.
15 William Gass, *On Being Blue* (Manchester, 1979), pp. 73, 75–6.
16 Susan Aldworth's description of the brain, in a diary entry describing her experience of a cerebral angiogram, 26 October 2001. See www.susanaldworth.com.

Brainscape 30 2006 etching and aquatint 50 x 35 cms

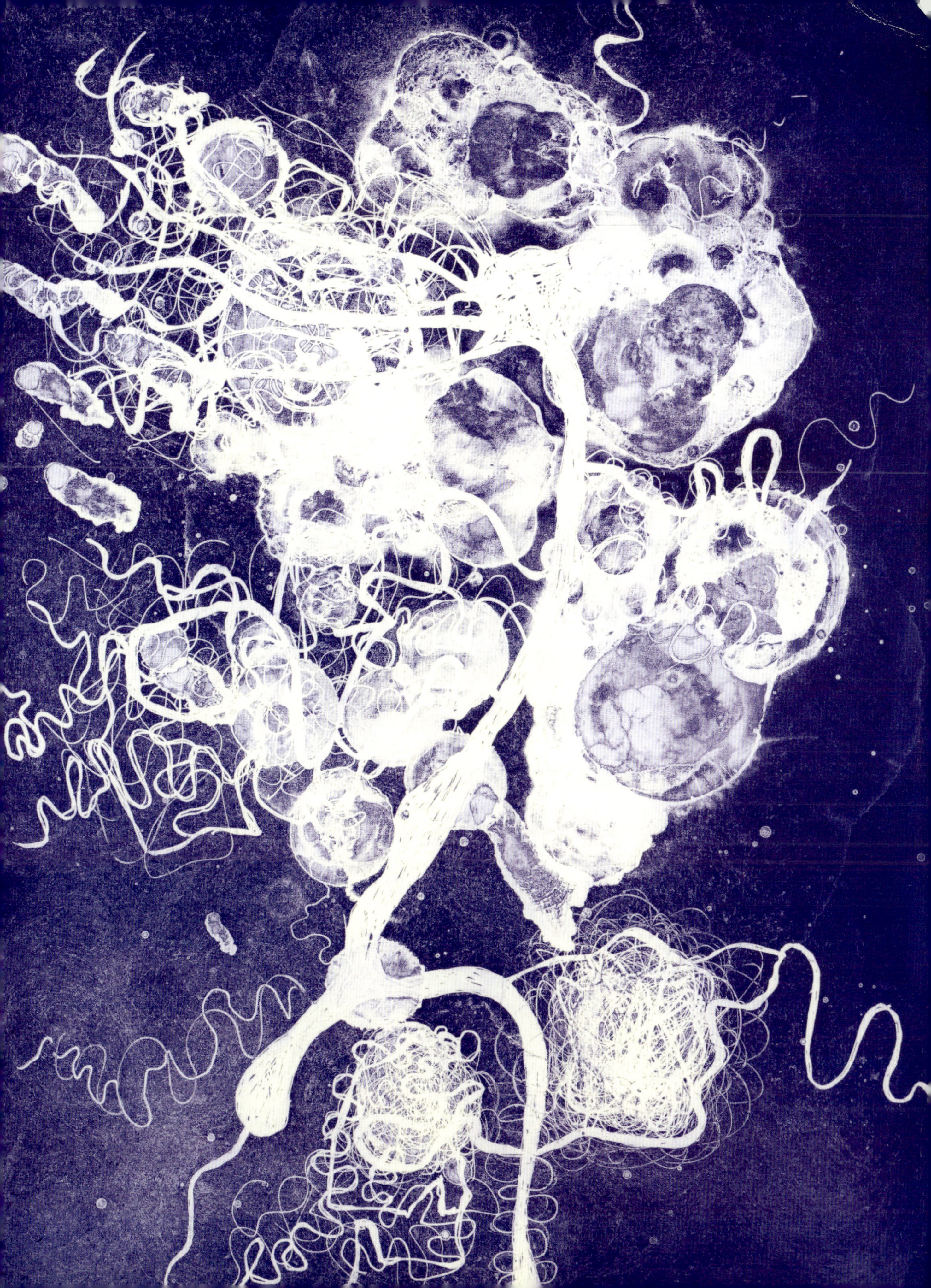

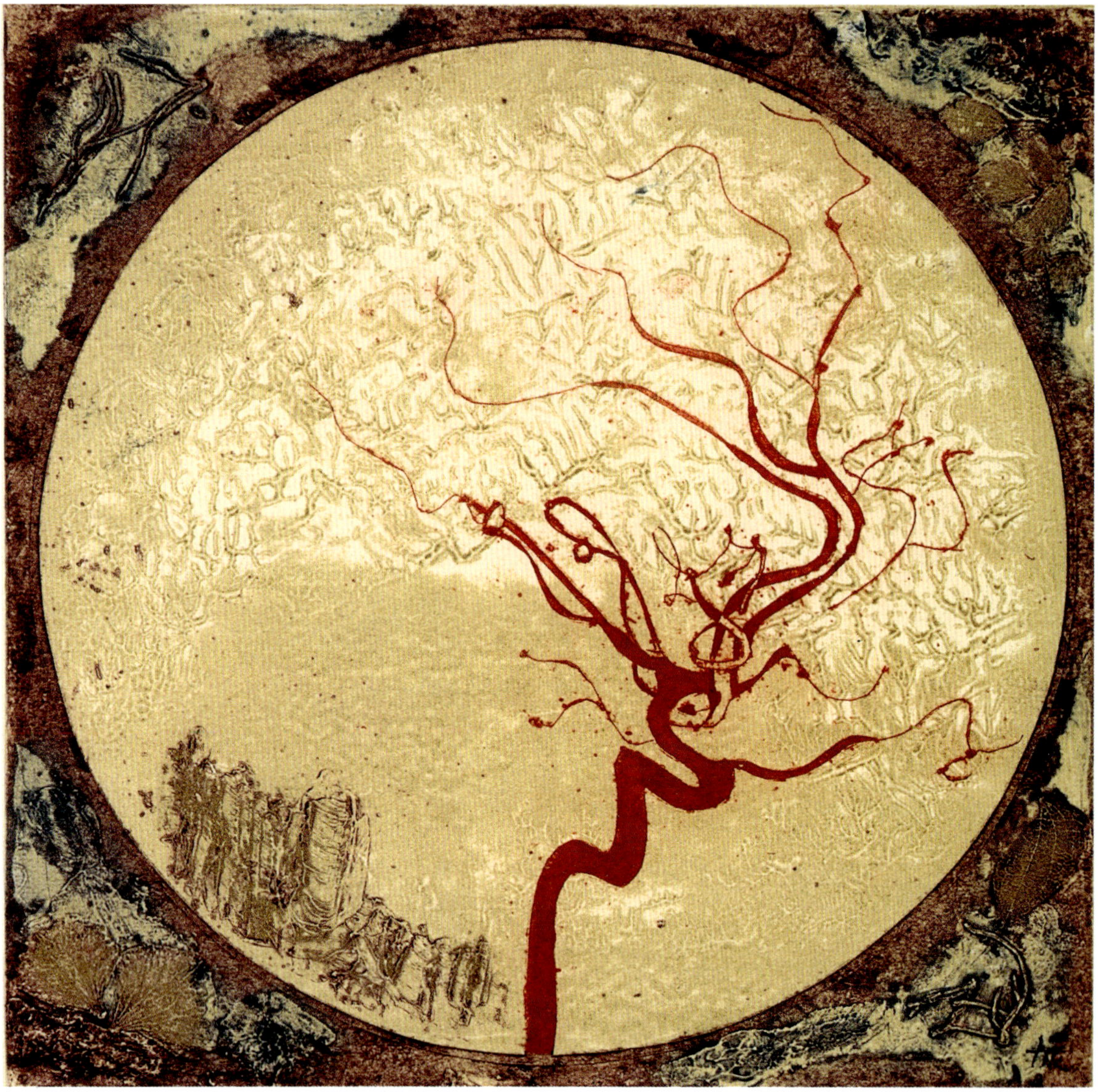

PAUL BROKS

INFANT FINGERS

The most beautiful experience we can have is the mysterious. It is the fundamental emotion that stands at the cradle of true art and true science.

Albert Einstein, *The World As I See It*

INFANT FINGERS ARE INCLINED to pick at the tightest philosophical knots. As matters of social identity are settled (*Who am I?*) so more obstinate questions arise (the *Whats* and the *Whys*). I remember, when I was about seven years old, staring transfixed at my fingers. Clearly these objects were a part of my body but did it make any sense to imagine that they were a part of *me*? I could control them, but then I could control a bicycle or a fishing rod and if I lost the bike or the rod I would still be me; likewise if I lost the fingers, or a foot. So what exactly was the relationship between my body and me? Where in the machinery was that thinking, observing 'I'? Susan Aldworth's work is about the mystery of consciousness. It shares the same innocence.

If you are not tantalized by the problem of consciousness then either you have solved it or you have not understood it in the first place. Our bodies are mostly invisible. We never see internal organs in the living flesh, and regions not hidden are, moment by moment, largely absent to awareness. Eyes closed, you can conjure a spectral image of the body (of 'yourself'), locating limbs, torso and head, tuning in to warmth and cold, aches, itches and muscular tensions, the rise and fall of the rib cage. But the spectre you invoke flickers and fades. The bodily sensorium is an unstable medium, part objective observation, part imaginative construction. Mostly the machinery takes care of itself. A cracked fingernail or infected tooth will bellow for attention but the body's default position is silence. We prefer to think of ourselves as ghosts. Now here's the paradox: the zone of deepest silence is the brain. Three pounds or so of jellified fats, proteins and sugars packed into the bony box of the skull, numb and dark as a tomb. But look at the spirits summoned up from the sludge. Look at the carnival of consciousness that flows from the void. How is this possible?

Between a Thing and a Thought 2000 collagraph printed from two plates 20 x 20 cms

A distinguished philosopher of mind once told me that to contemplate the great problems of philosophy was almost to engage in a physical confrontation. Deep thought was visceral, and to say that one was 'wrestling' or 'grappling' with a problem was more than empty metaphor. Aldworth's art springs from a visceral contemplation of this, the deepest problem of all: *How does matter become mind?* Her concern, as an artist, is to embrace the emotional and aesthetic dimensions of the question itself, recapturing the voltage surge of awe and bewilderment felt when, during a medical procedure, she was faced with radiological images of the interior of her own head, real time. *You are thinking about what you are seeing with what you are seeing on the screen.* This is the mind/body problem stripped to the bone. The mission of science and philosophy is to dispel the paradox; Aldworth celebrates it. Her work brings another twist to the spiral. If one function of art is to intensify consciousness – of feelings, images, ideas – then, with consciousness itself under scrutiny, the relationship of form and content comes close to collapse. The fusion of image and idea sends us tumbling to the brink of an infinite regress, chasing consciousness of consciousness of consciousness of consciousness ...

This is the Century of Neuroscience. Images of the brain have become commonplace. Textbooks and websites show us photographs of real brains extracted from the cranium, cling-wrapped in slimy membranes, arteries squirming like earthworms through the ruts and ridges below. We see half-brains precision-sliced to display pristine structures within, neat as fossils. Then there's the anatomical art: skulls opened like hatches to reveal brains *in situ* (the face below usually passive, not even mildly surprised); three-dimensional cutaways are colour-coded and signposted to guide us through the vaults and chambers, the pathways, canals and aqueducts of the labyrinthine city of the soul. Modern neuroimaging methods – PET, fMRI, MEG – bring the metropolis to life. Trails of colour trace the circuitries of memory and emotion. We see thought turning to intention, intention to action with the changing of the cerebral lights. We can even distinguish the signatures of truth and deceit, written in blood, or rather patterns of blood flow, across the cortical mantle. Do we need more pictures of the brain? For Aldworth, such images, the real and the hyper-real, the photographic and the digital, are deeply provocative but serve only to intensify the core ambiguities that drive her work. The harder one

A Penny for Your Thoughts 2002 mixed media 43 x 35 cms

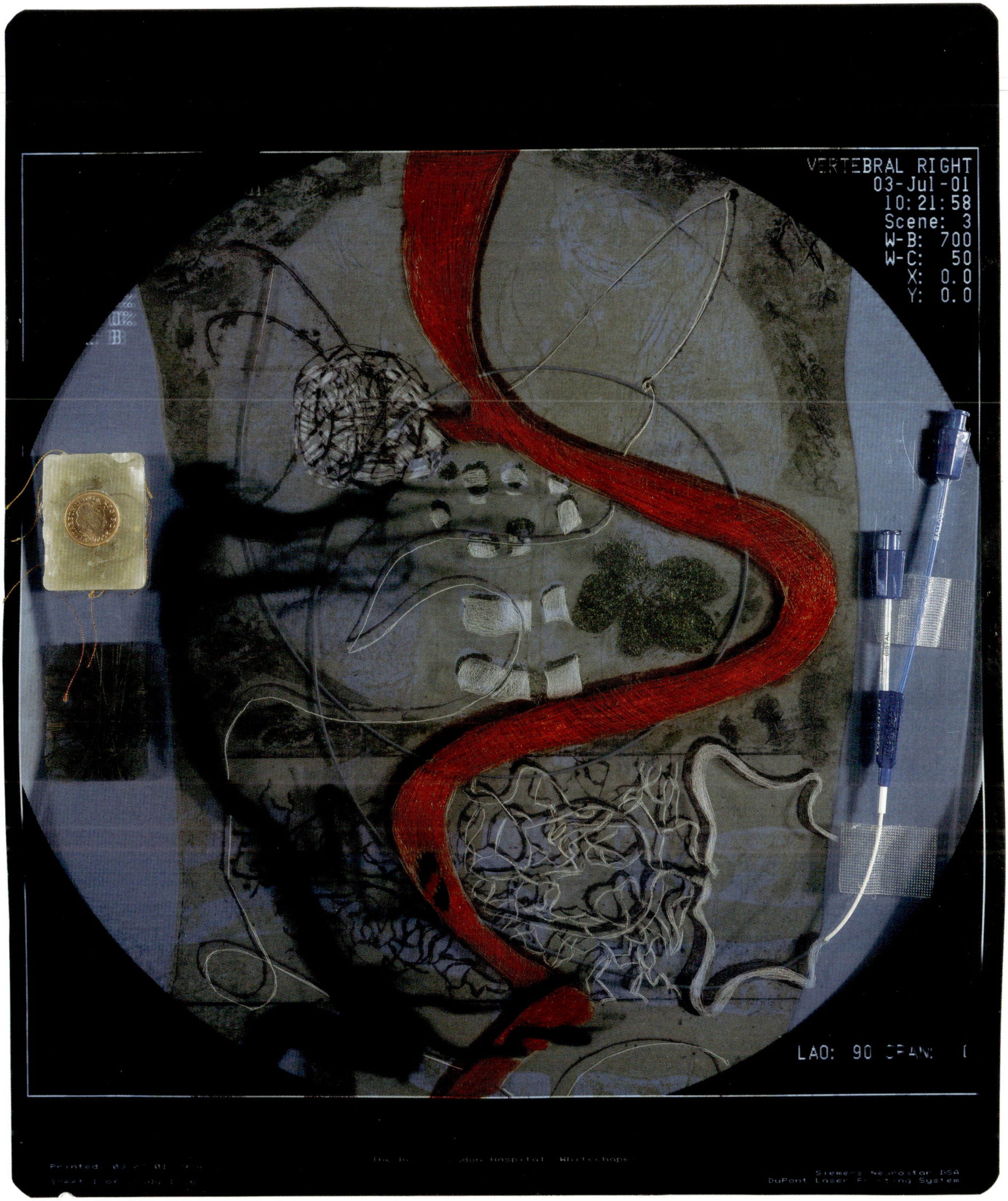
VERTEBRAL RIGHT
03-Jul-01
10:21:58
Scene: 3
W-B: 700
W-C: 50
X: 0.0
Y: 0.0
LAO: 90

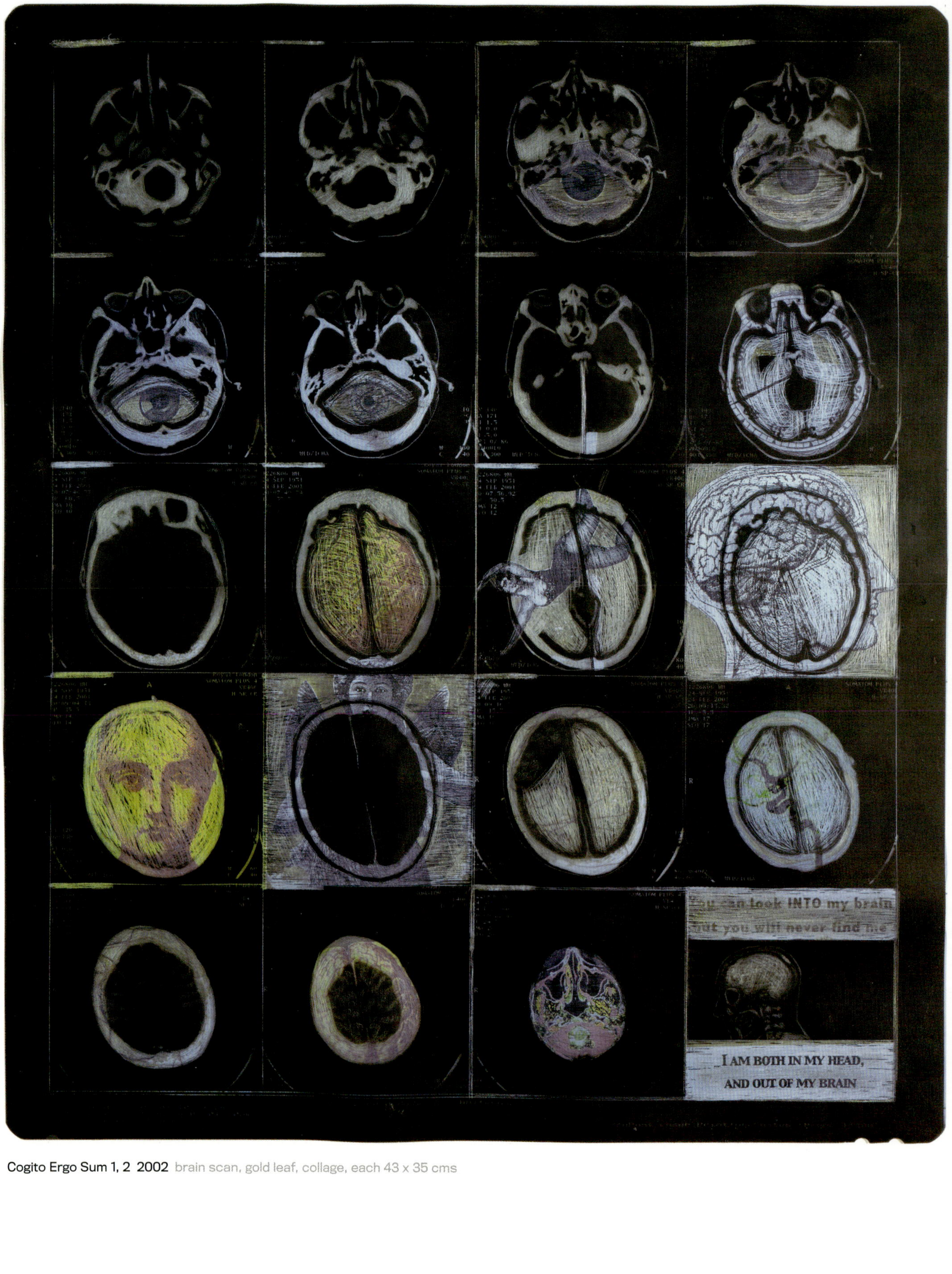

Cogito Ergo Sum 1, 2 2002 brain scan, gold leaf, collage, each 43 x 35 cms

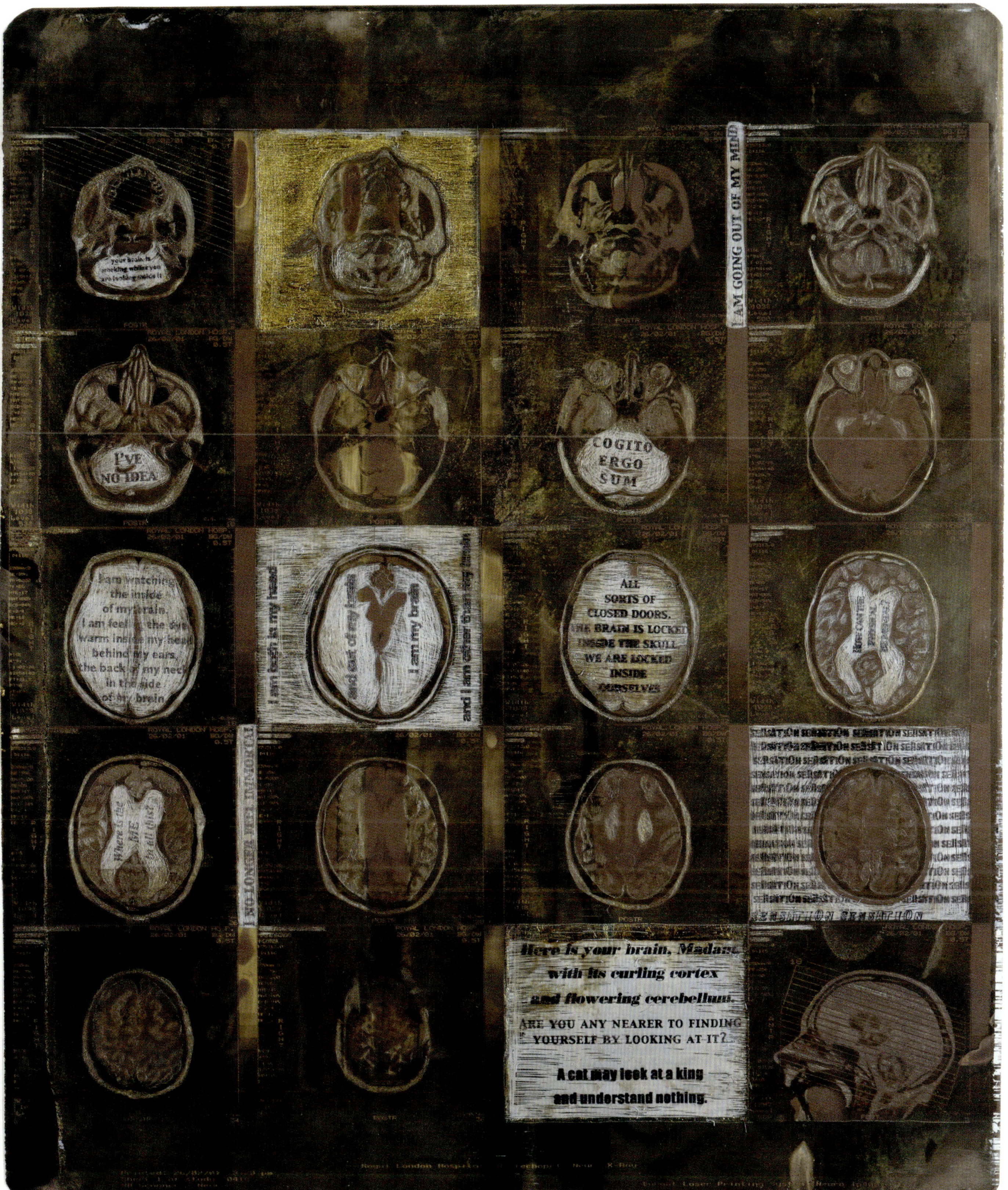
working while you
I AM GOING OUT OF MY MIND
I'VE NO IDEA
COGITO ERGO SUM
I am watching the inside of my brain. I am feeling the dye warm inside my head behind my ears, the back of my neck in the side of my brain
I am both in my head
and out of my head
I am my brain
and I am other than my brain
ALL SORTS OF CLOSED DOORS. THE BRAIN IS LOCKED INSIDE THE SKULL. WE ARE LOCKED INSIDE OURSELVES
Where is the ME in all this
I NO LONGER FEEL IMMORTAL
SENSATION SENSATION
Here is your brain, Madam, with its curling cortex and flowering cerebellum.
ARE YOU ANY NEARER TO FINDING YOURSELF BY LOOKING AT IT?
A cat may look at a king and understand nothing.

stares into the machinery of the brain, the starker the realisation that *there is no one in there*. There is no inner sanctum of the self. Neural networks have a life and logic of their own. There is no one running the show. The self is a shadow-puppet shaped by the firings of a hundred billion brain cells. These are conceptual conundrums. Intractable to current science, they call for an artistic response.

Drawing and painting in operating theatres and angiography suites, Aldworth derives inspiration from the dynamics of medical procedure as much as from the components of the visual scene. But if her work is representative of an ancient tradition of artists working alongside anatomists and physicians, it also reflects contemporary trends. Neuroscience is emerging as one of the grand belief systems informing the imagination of artists and writers in the twenty-first century, just as Marxism and the psychodynamic theories of Freud and Jung stamped their mark on the art of the twentieth. Conversely, science has become interested in art. The grand mission of neuroscience is to chart the neural infrastructure of the human mind and there is no reason to exempt artistic experience. Through the new discipline of 'neuroaesthetics' the cognitive apparatus of art will be 'reverse-engineered' as surely as the machineries of memory, language and emotion are being dismantled. Or perhaps not. It may turn out that by setting out to explain art, science will do no more than mark its own limits. To engage with a work of art is to absorb its meanings at a personal level and so, like consciousness itself, the experience has elements that are irreducibly subjective. Science doesn't go there. I have made a career in neuropsychology, studying the structures and functions of the brain. I stand in awe at the vertiginous progress of modern neuroscience, but still I'm staring at my fingers.

Matter into Imagination 3, 4 2006 perspex plate on collagraph plate, each 41 x 58 cms

overleaf: Apoptosis 4 2007 etching and aquatint 35 x 50 cms

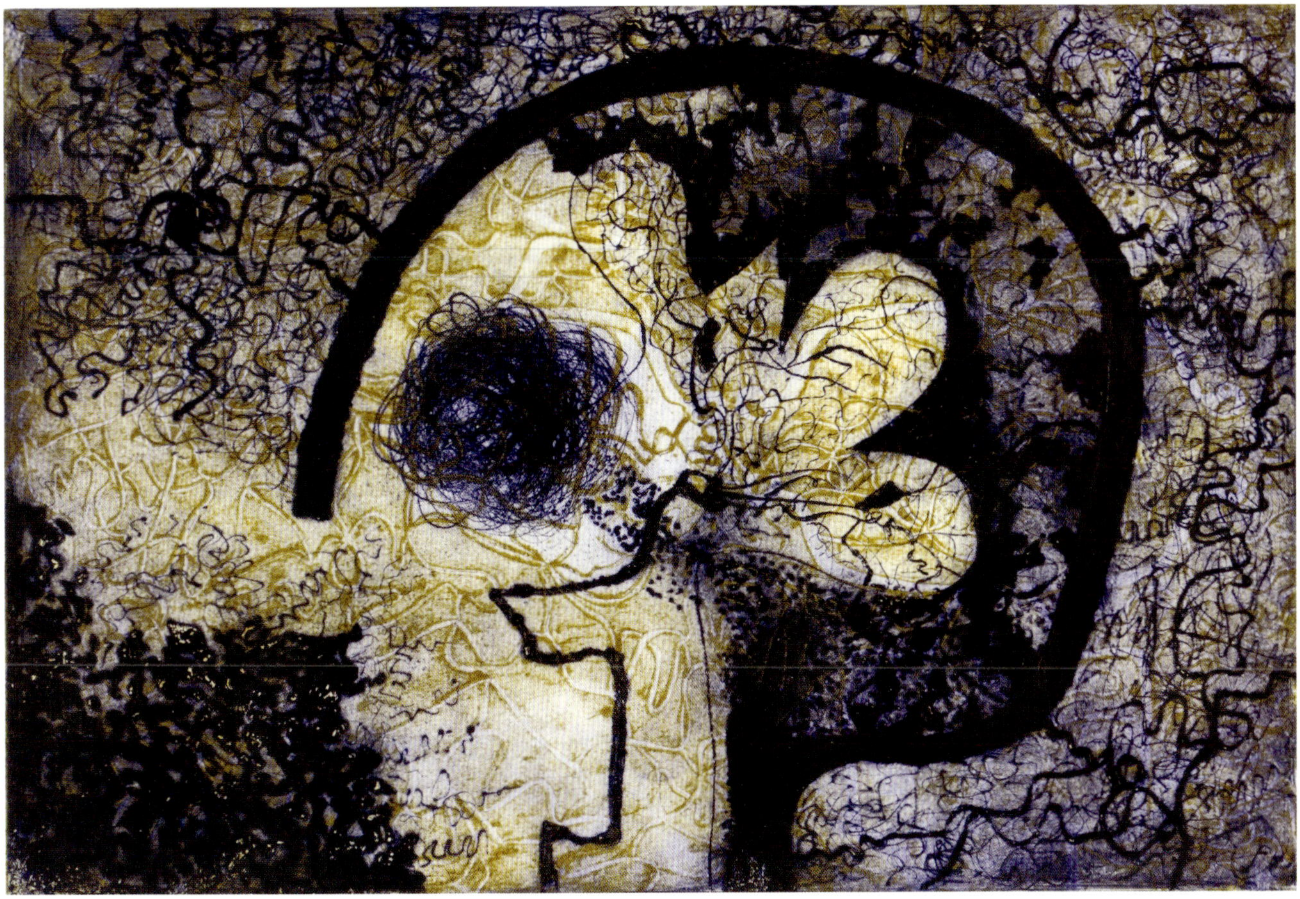

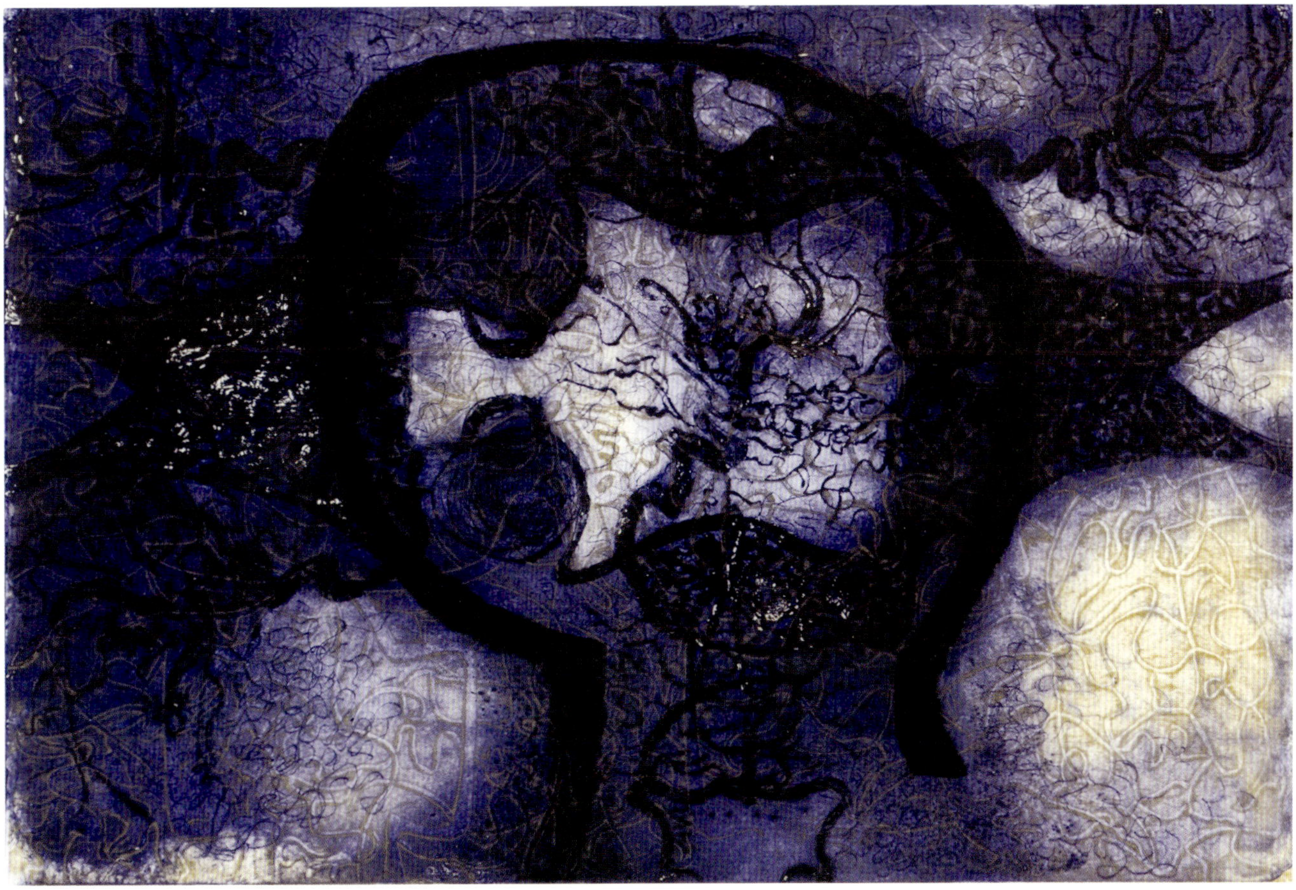

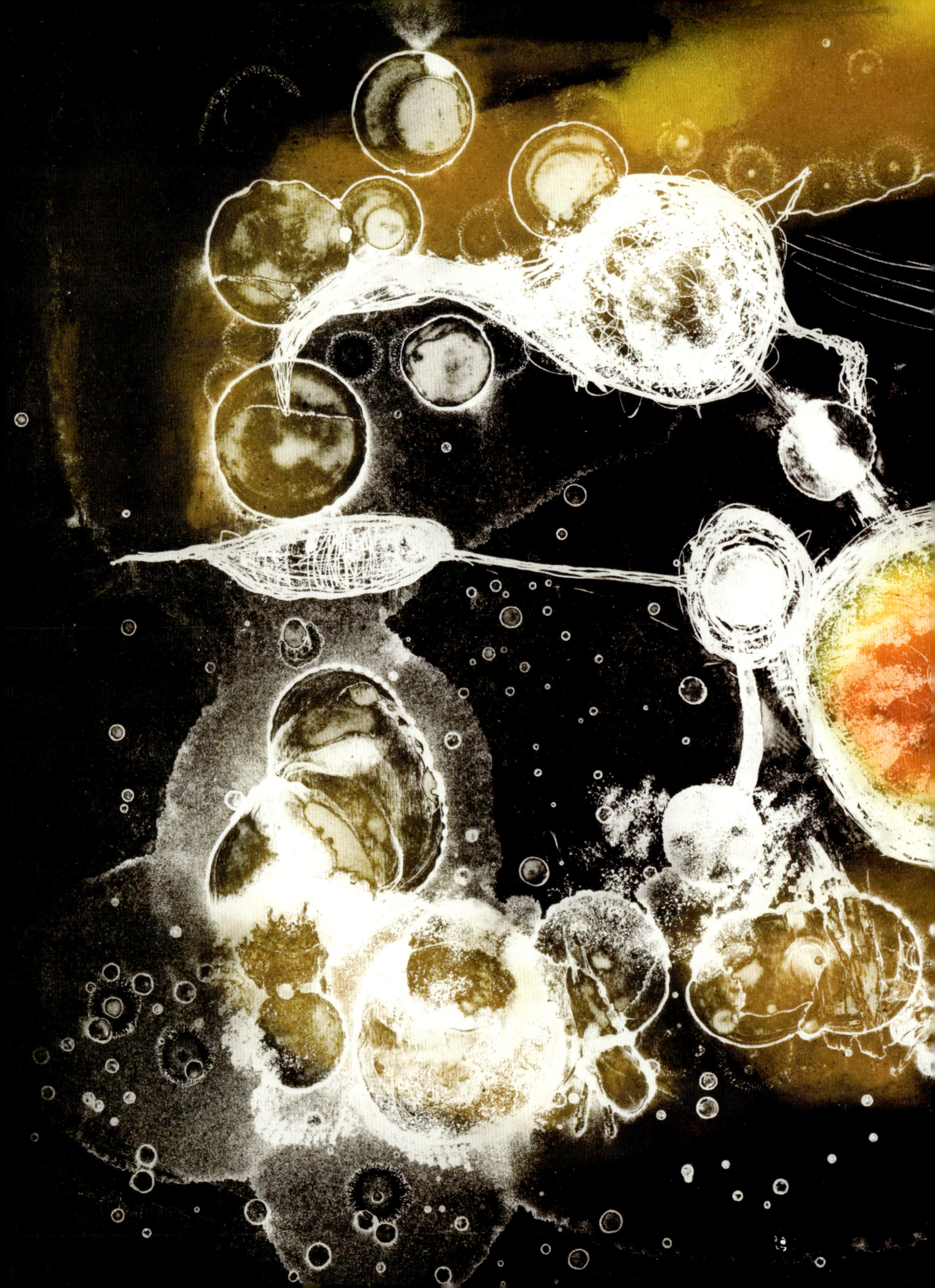

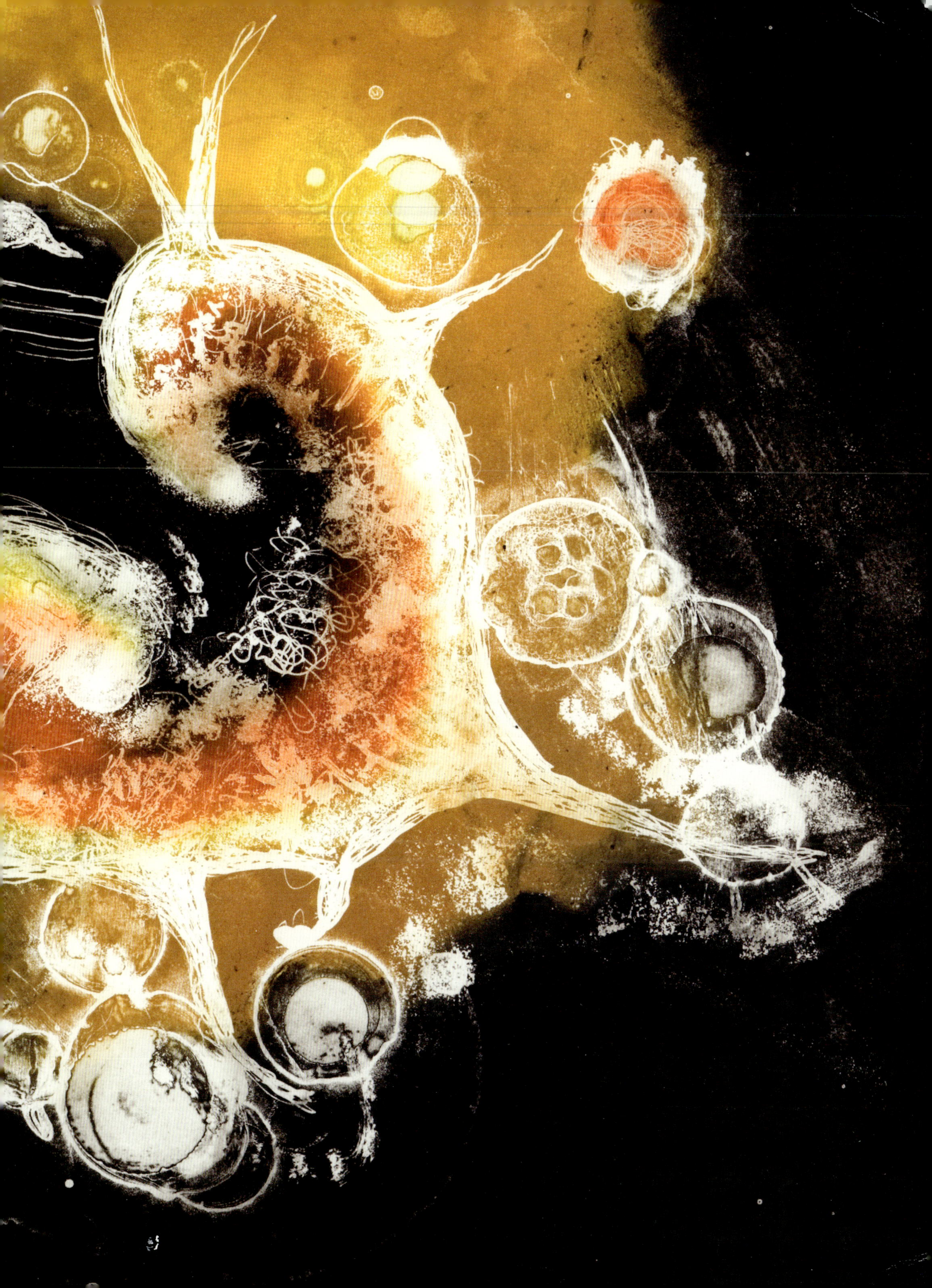

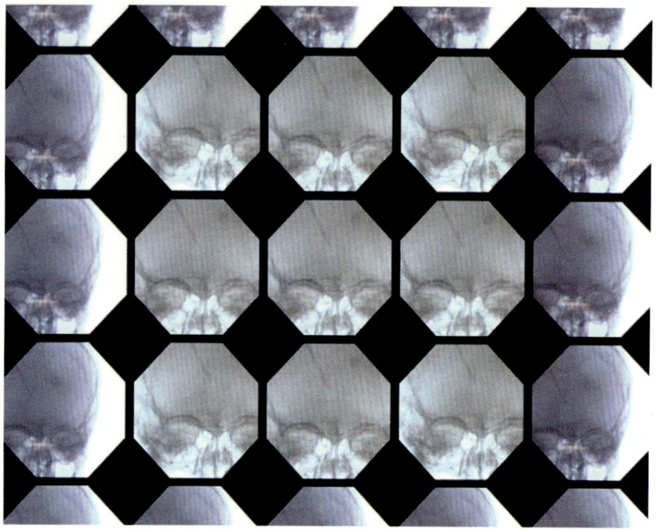
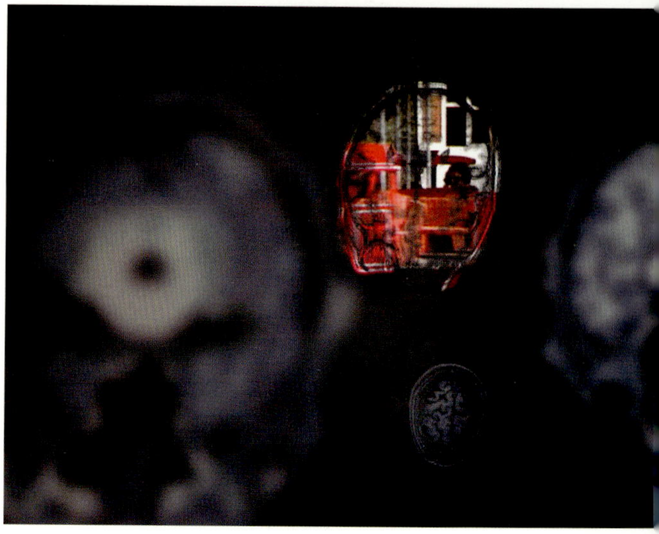
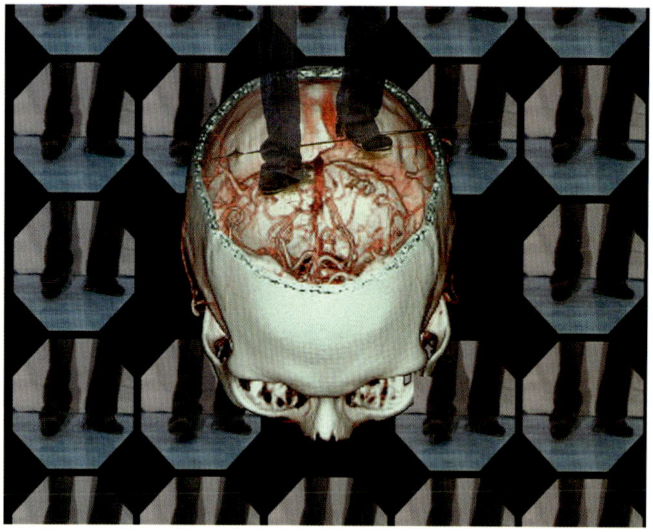
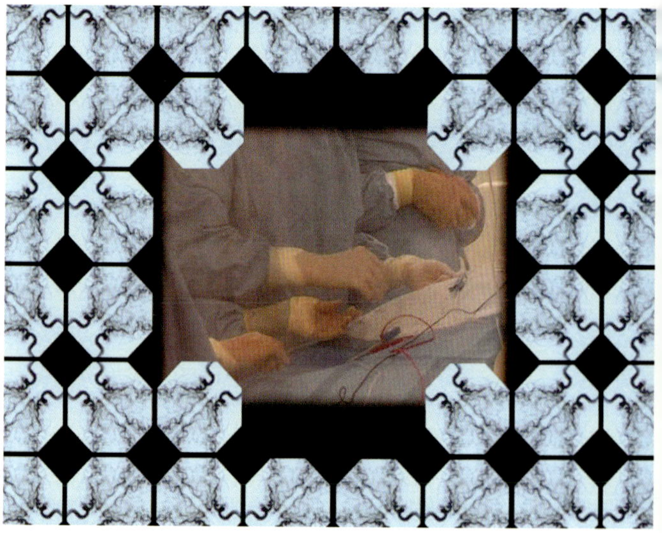
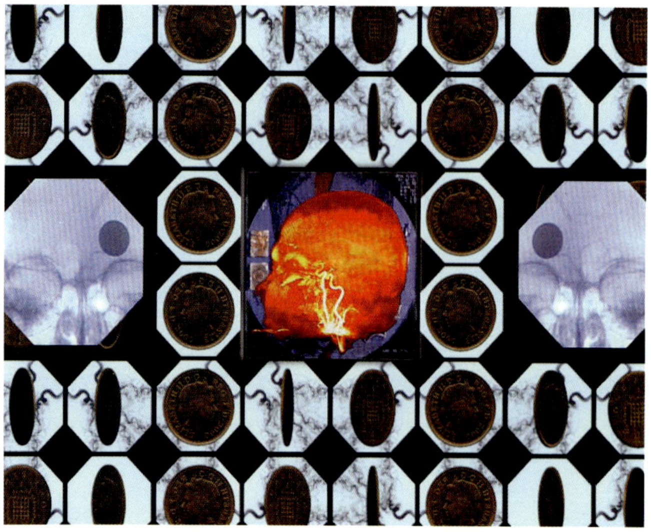
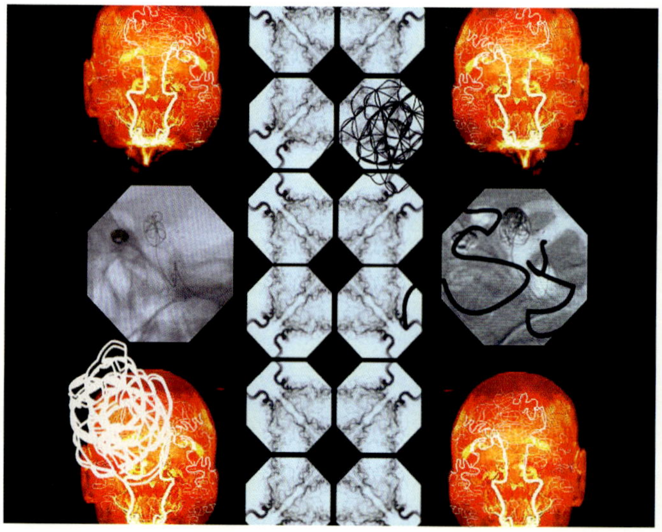

Going Native 2006 film

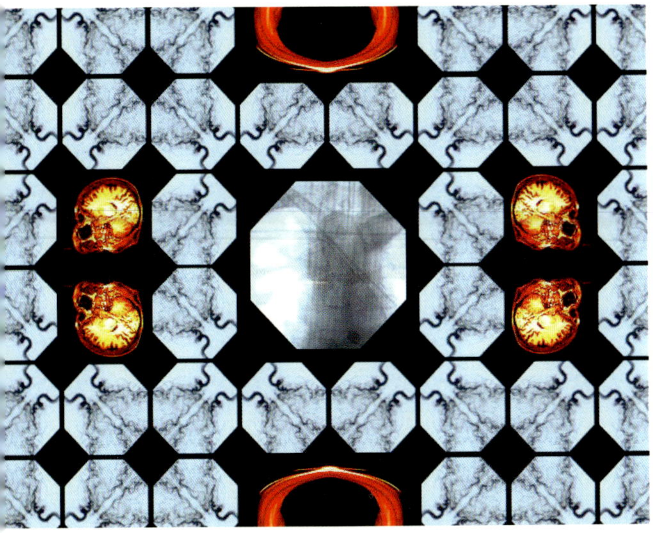
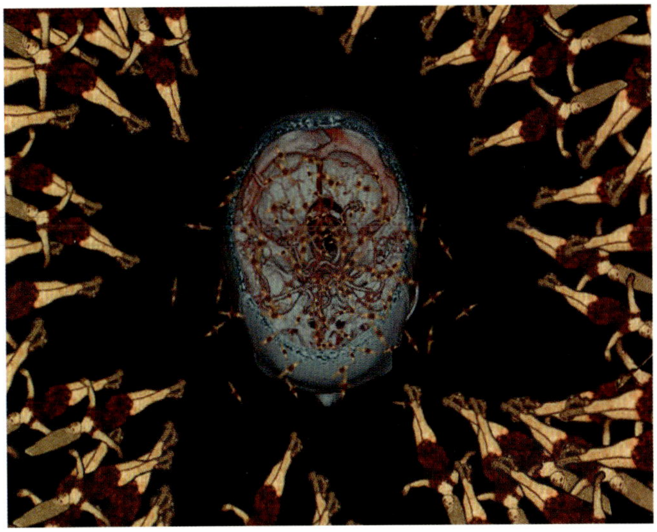
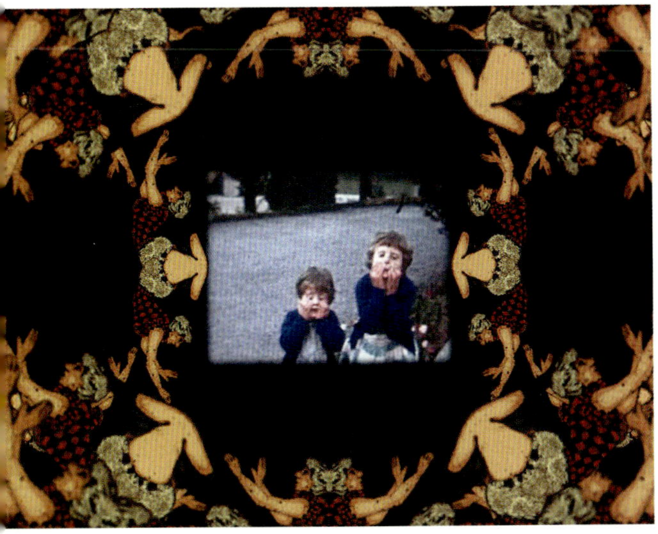
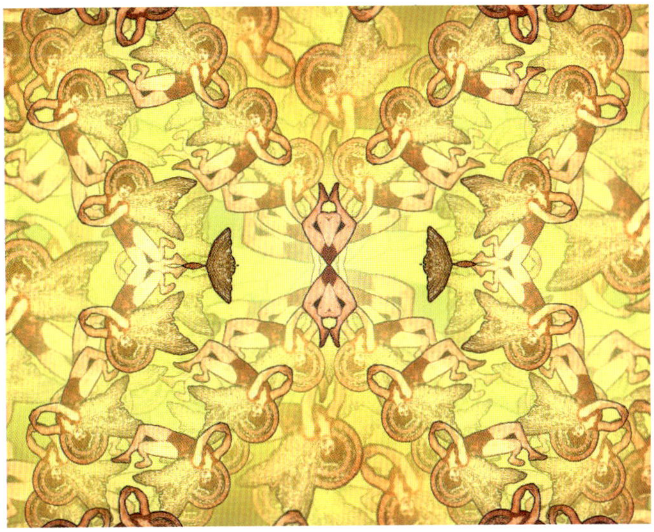
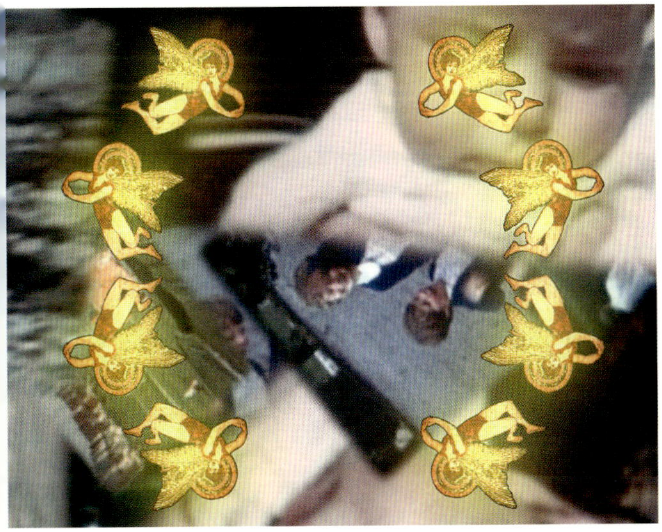
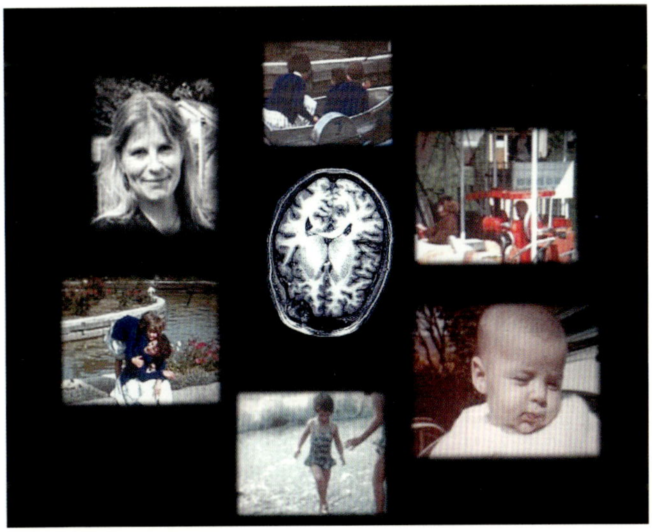

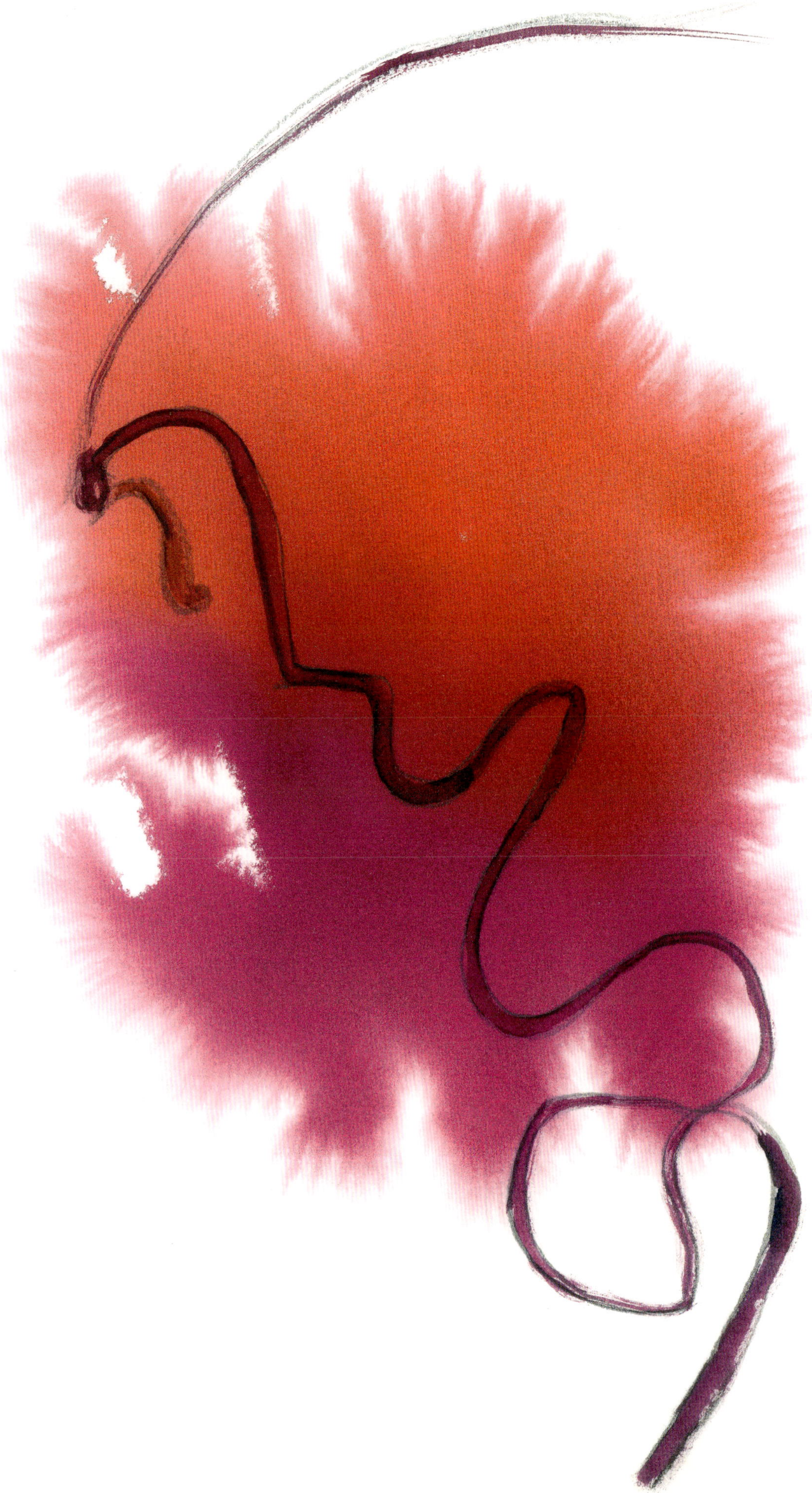

ROBERT MASON

MATERIAL MYSTERIES

GREAT MYSTERIES INVITE US to rationalise or celebrate them, and artists are inevitably drawn to this process. Susan Aldworth's chosen mystery centres on 'the material nature of personal identity', and her work has involved her in a longstanding dialogue with medicine and science – especially, neuroscience. More specifically, this dialogue focuses on the human body: her own body and other people's bodies.

Historically, Western artists placed the religious impulse, at once so attractive and so destructive, at the centre of their work. At the behest of the Church, their art revolved for many centuries around the mysteries of existence – creation, (im)mortality and morality – striving, within the boundaries set by their patrons' belief systems and political agendas, to find expression for these profound themes.

Globally, art has echoed this 'striving', offering physical form to spiritual dilemmas that come cloaked in a bewildering array of theisms, hagiographies, and arcane (though everyday) rituals, derived from an equal confusion of sacred texts. The process has thrown up, as a positive complement to persecution, war, torture, terrorism and unrivalled social arrogance, some of our most beautiful and profound art forms – and not, obviously, just within the confines of drawing and painting. From Bach's sacred cantatas to an Andalucian crowd's passionate serenading of a carved Madonna during *Semana Santa*, and from austere Ethiopian stone churches to the intricate geometric dance of Islamic mosaics, the religious impulse has generated the transcendent and the terrifying, equally.

But for many contemporary artists, religion's negatives outweigh its positives, to the extent that it proves impossible to align their art with the formulae and speculative certainties of the religious search. An alternative lies in replacing one great mystery with another: for Aldworth, the mystery of the physical self – especially, the brain – and its attendant metaphysical conundrums.

Location 4.1.06 acrylic ink and graphite 38 x 27 cms

It could be said that there is an *existential* enquiry occurring here, rather than a religious or spiritual one, since it is scaled down from the universal to the personal, and rooted far more in the material than in the mystical. Aldworth chooses a 'search' that is intimate and comprehensible rather than global and grandiose, well aware that we are all in the same boat, all locked in our own little one-person vessel with its imperfections, everyday miracles and inevitable sell-by date.

Such enquiry is not new within art, and historically it has often been undertaken in tandem with more conventionally religious imagery. It is tantalizing to look at Leonardo's unflinching anatomical research, taking place alongside his flawless religious commissions, and to speculate on the depth of his excitement about the two bodies of work. Or to consider Rembrandt's luminous Biblical masterpieces, and then *The Anatomy Lesson of Doctor Nicolaes Tulp*, or the small drawing, *Hanged Woman on a Gibbet*. Though Rembrandt's humanism and virtuosity shine through all his work, something about the awkwardness of that last image makes one suspect that the great human mystery of a life ended – stripped of religion's 'certainties' – affected him most profoundly. One could even apply this train of thought to his self-portraits, though – considered individually at least – they are not as literally concerned with mortality.

Within contemporary art, the enquiry into corporeal experience has many outcomes. Marlene Dumas's and Jenny Saville's paintings share a direct lineage with Rembrandt's humanism, as do Michael Landy's powerfully unsentimental drawings of his dying father. Helen Chadwick's mandala-like assemblages, juxtaposing human and industrial materials, embody a search for meaning that reaches beyond what they actually depict. Andres Serrano and Joel-Peter Witkin exploit photography's directness to extraordinary effect. The shamanistic experiments of Franko B, Otto Muehl and Orlan push a concern with physicality into areas that some find hard even to categorise as 'art', though physical extremes have often been part of the mystic's experience: that religious impulse, again.

Aldworth's art inhabits a less confrontational, though no less serious realm. Her involvement in working from the body and addressing notions of consciousness and personality is longstanding. It stems from a traumatic personal experience – one might almost say a 'conversion' of sorts – but she has moved her work away from egocentricity to something more altruistic

Apoptosis 1, 2 2007 etching and aquatint, each 35 x 50 cms

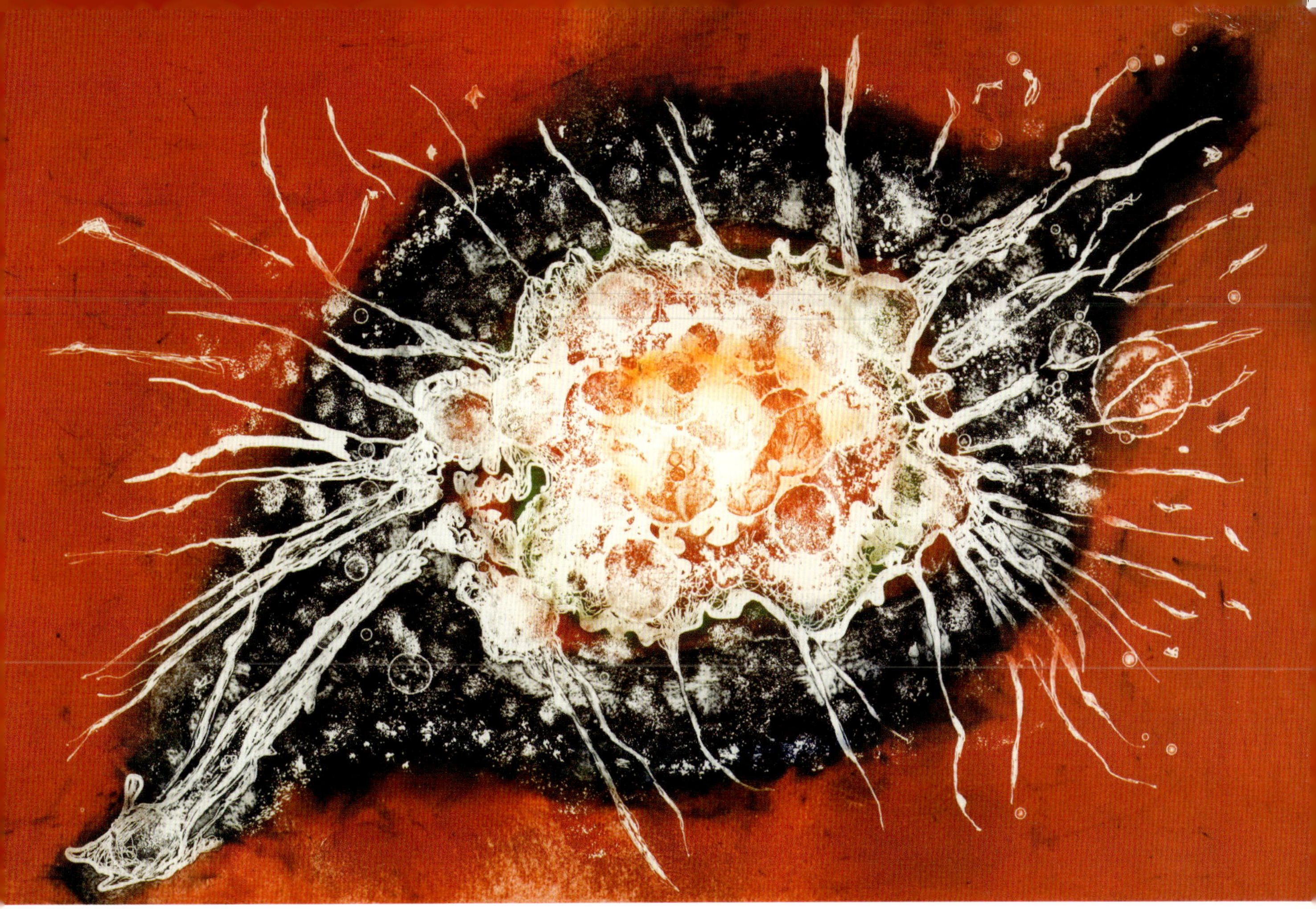

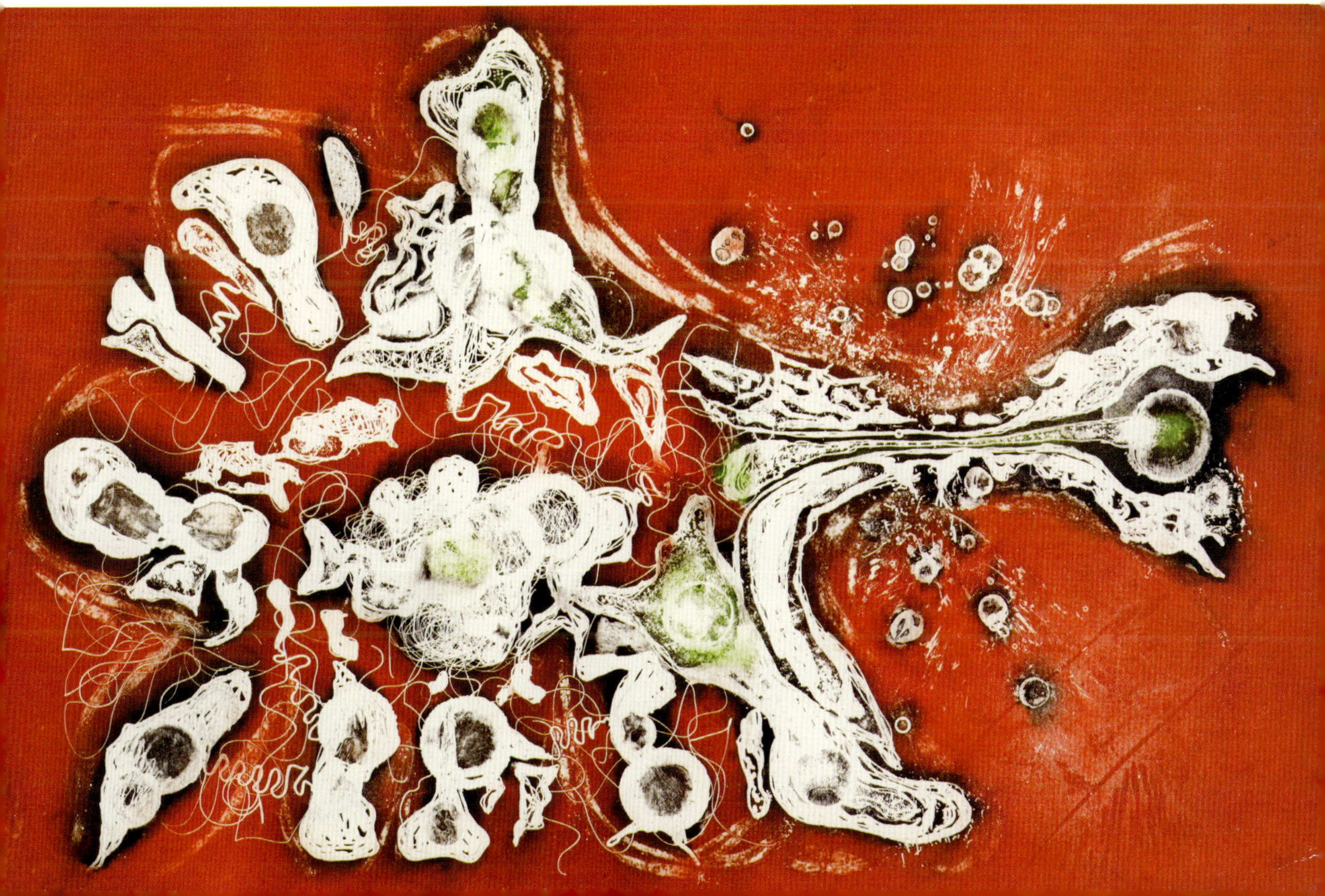

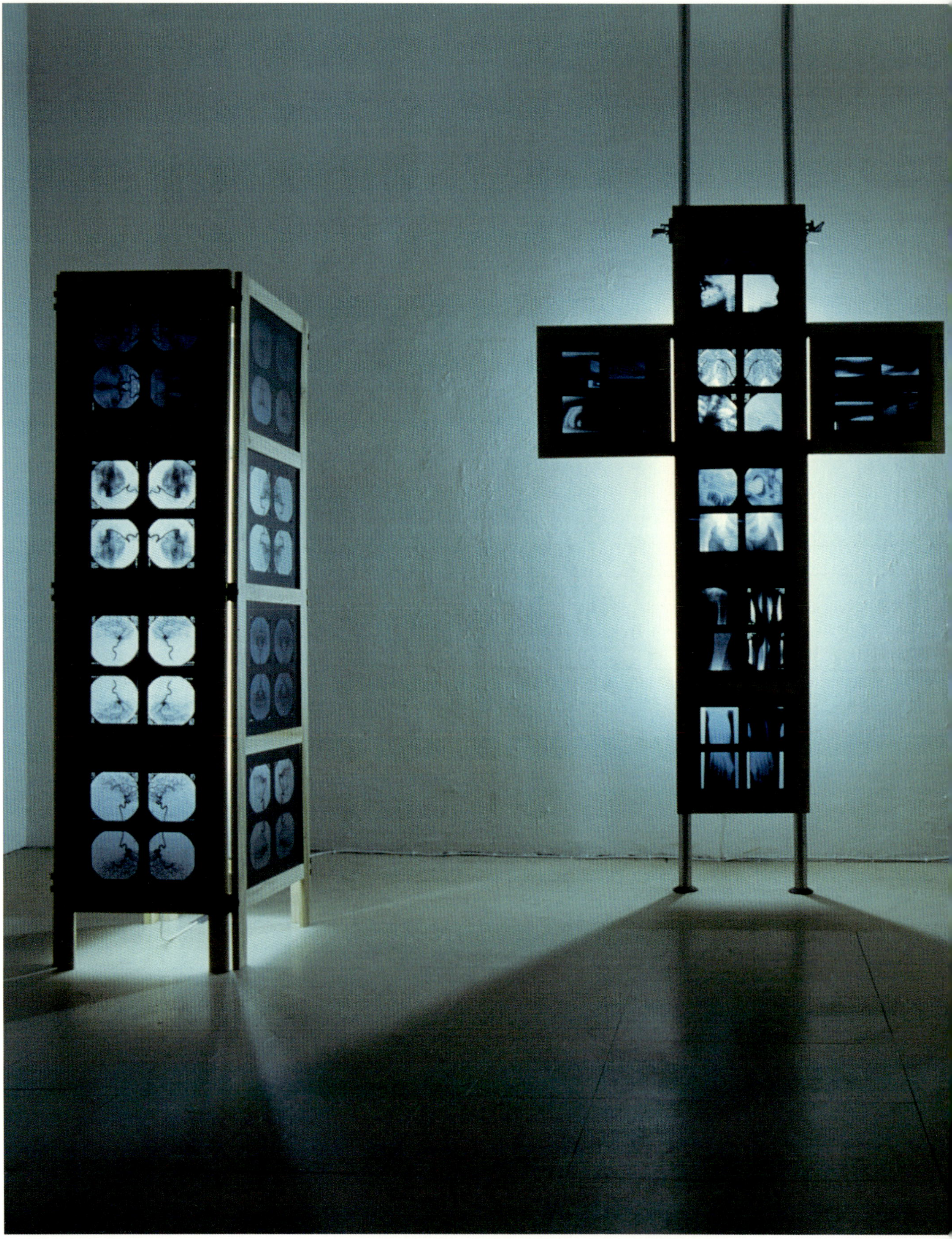

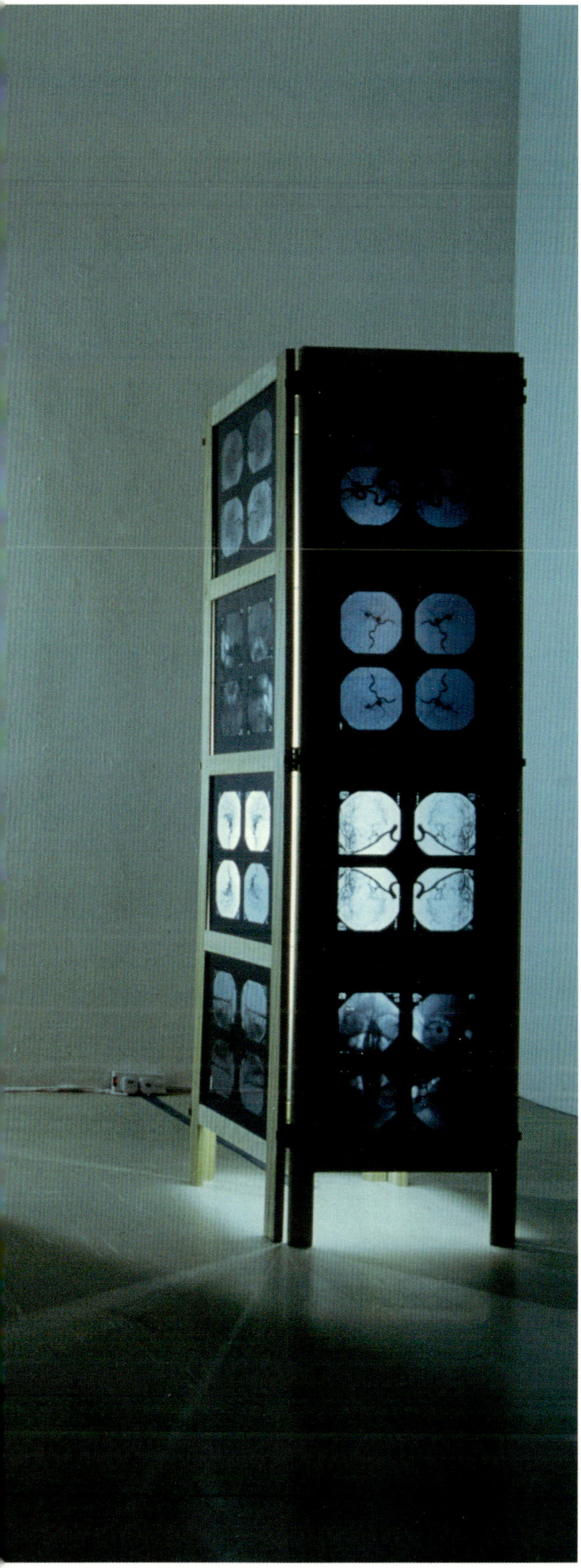

Hinged Crucifix and Plinths 2002
installation at Whitechapel Gallery

and generous. In doing so she has involved an equally generous range of processes and media, collaborating with digital artists, musicians, wood workers and printmakers, while keeping intact a firm sense of direction.

As well as artistic collaborators, Aldworth has engaged with surgeons, psychologists, academics – and crucially, with patients themselves – to create a sense of shared humanity that runs through her output. This aspect of her work makes her part of the humanist lineage mentioned earlier: Aldworth's concerns may revolve around identity, but they are neither solipsistic nor isolationist.

If any artist embodies such a humanist tradition it is surely Rembrandt, and it is notable that Aldworth has chosen a medium inevitably identified with him as the vehicle for her most recent work. But etching's literal penetration of a surface not only links her with creative precursors; it also, intentionally or otherwise, chimes in with notions of penetrating – entering – the body (and even the 'self', whatever that is): notions that Aldworth has seen physically enacted, scores of times, during surgical procedures.

And her own body becomes an element in this scribing process: as part of the making of a piece she has to expose parts of her self to the aquatint process; hooded in plastic, she is unable to breathe as resin dust settles on her, and an image of her hand or arm is transposed onto the plate. What appears on the wall, as a two-dimensional image, is actually a record of a more demanding physical experience.

In the light of her serious concerns, it is perhaps surprising that a certain element of playfulness is apparent in Aldworth's work. Its presence is partly due to the process of exploration and discovery involved in the making of the plates themselves: as well as the work being physically hard, it is genuinely *exciting*, and this excitement finds a path into the prints.

But there is a further refreshing sense of near-frivolity in some of the images. A disembodied hand balances a disembodied brain on one finger like a pizza chef twirling dough, while sperm-like oscillating interneurons undulate as if choreographed by some microscopic Busby Berkeley. Frenetic scored marks, derived from arteries, veins, shunts and catheters, evolve into flower shapes, amoebic forms, and graffiti that strive to tell us something in a language that the writer is only partly fluent in, and that is foreign but attractive to us. Abstract smears of aquatint evoke the Milky Way, swarms of fireflies, or imagined creatures.

No Ghost in the Machine 2004 lightboxes with detail

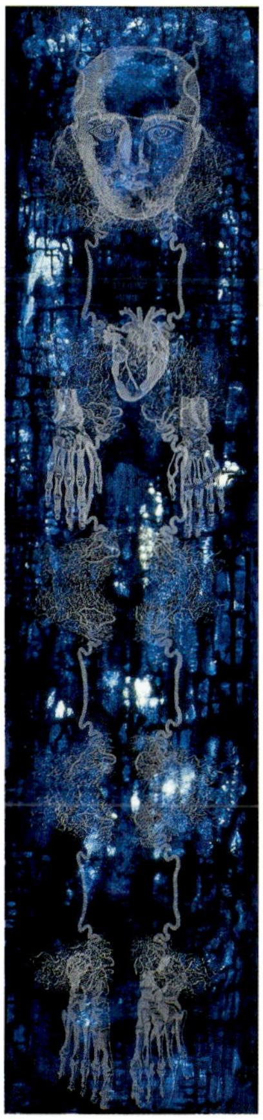

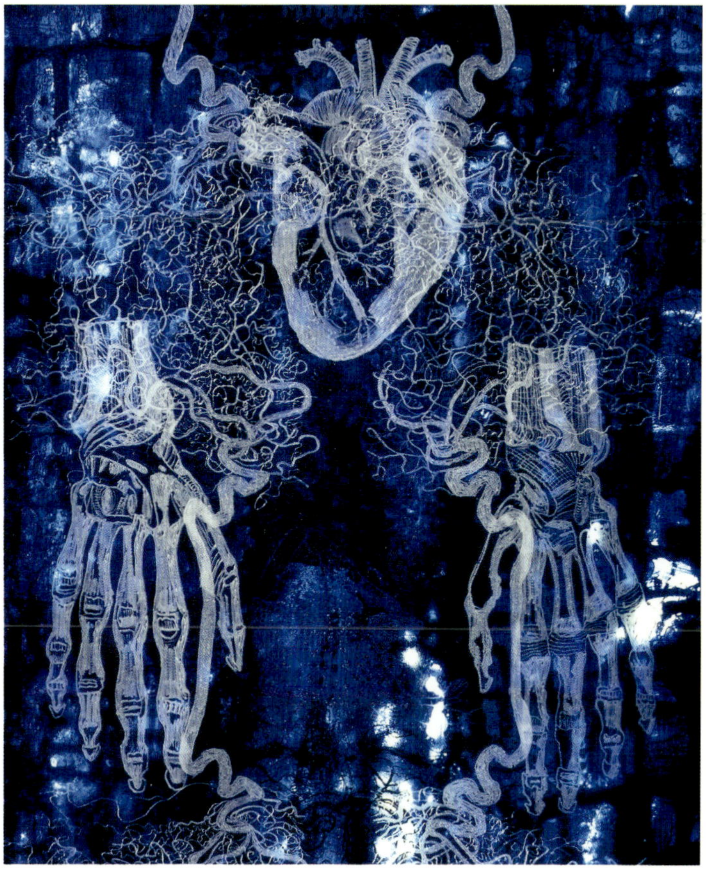

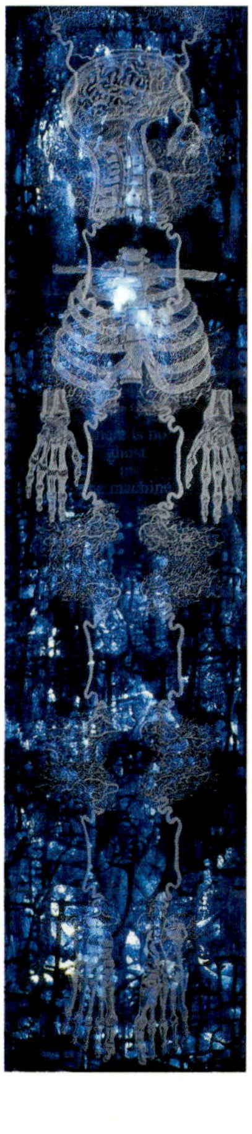

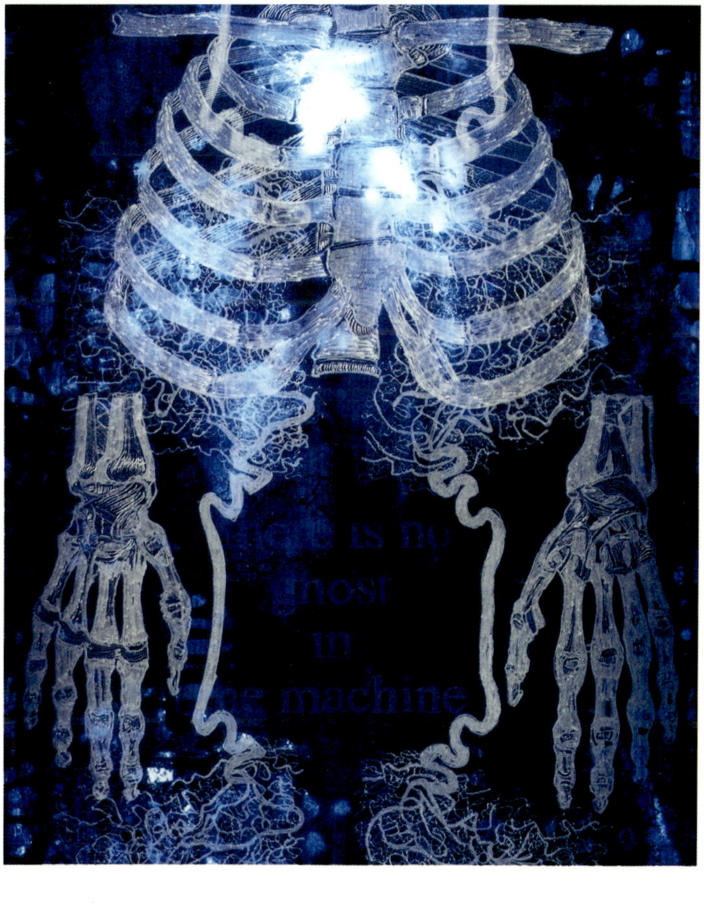

The potential sombreness of largely monochrome imagery, made in an antique process carrying centuries of import and precedent, is enlivened by a sense of discovery that celebrates the joys of thinking, feeling, working and sharing, and that is unusual in a period of irony and materialism within the arts.

Looking back once more, such 'playfulness' is not so surprising. Those involved with the visual exploration of the body have often imported a sense of embellishment and decoration into their images. Renaissance and Enlightenment dissection figures gesture heroically or camply in what must be malodorous Elysian Fields, sporting their skins like togas or peeling them back with optimistic coquettishness. The flawless anatomical figures of the seventeenth and eighteenth centuries present us with pearl tears on luscious, even eroticised wax 'skin', intended to make inner truths more palatable, or more shocking. Ruysch's preserved embryos sport natty lace collars, bracelets and anklets, while Honoré Fragonard's caper skittishly for eternity in his biblical tableaux.

Such embellishment conveys a loaded, even perverse mood in the face of death, but Aldworth's interest lies in vivacity, not in morbidity. Her work is rooted in observing and drawing a process of healing, rather than post-mortem dissection. Though a sense of seriousness is rightly present, and though we know that those attempts at healing might fail, a more positive atmosphere pervades things. The making of the work is part and parcel of present, shared existence: something to be relished, questioned and understood (as far as is possible). This is a process that engages intuition as much as intellect; the fact that the 'understanding' will probably always remain partial does not discount the value of the enquiry. We see here not a dressing-up of unpalatable mortality, but a response to the complex mysteries of *living* within this astonishing little 'one-person vessel'.

Paul Broks writes that 'The mission of science is to dispel the paradox [inherent in the mind/body problem]; Aldworth celebrates it'. In doing so, she contributes to a body of research and knowledge that needs its subjective aspects alongside the empirical: scientists of all stripes acknowledge this. She combines a genuine humanism with a liberated response to those mysteries that a more commonplace religious response reduces to stale formulae. There are, thankfully, no 'certainties' in her art, save for the fact that she is here, doing it, now, and we are here to respond to it.

Shadow Puppet 6 2007 etching and aquatint 50 x 35 cms

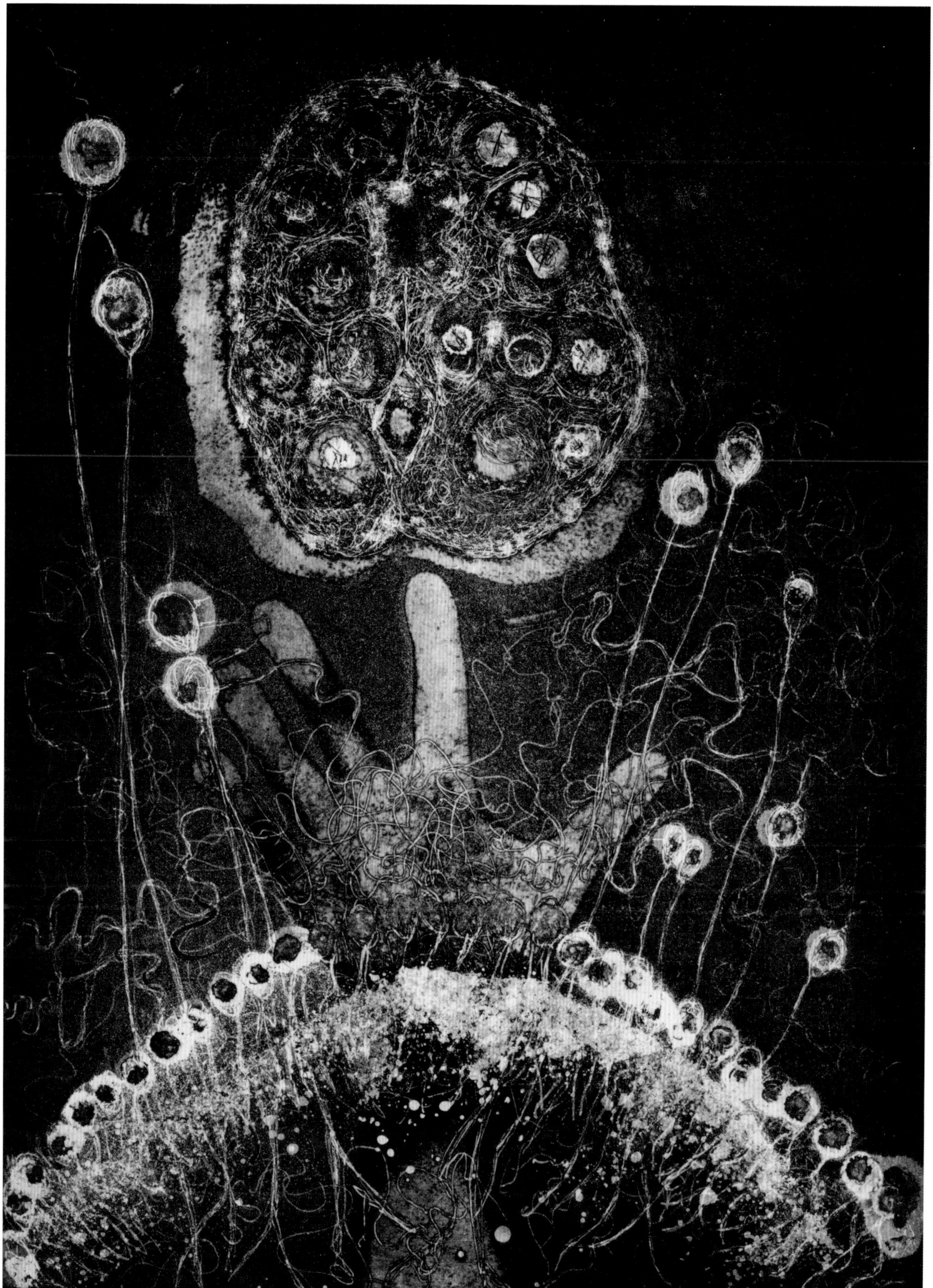

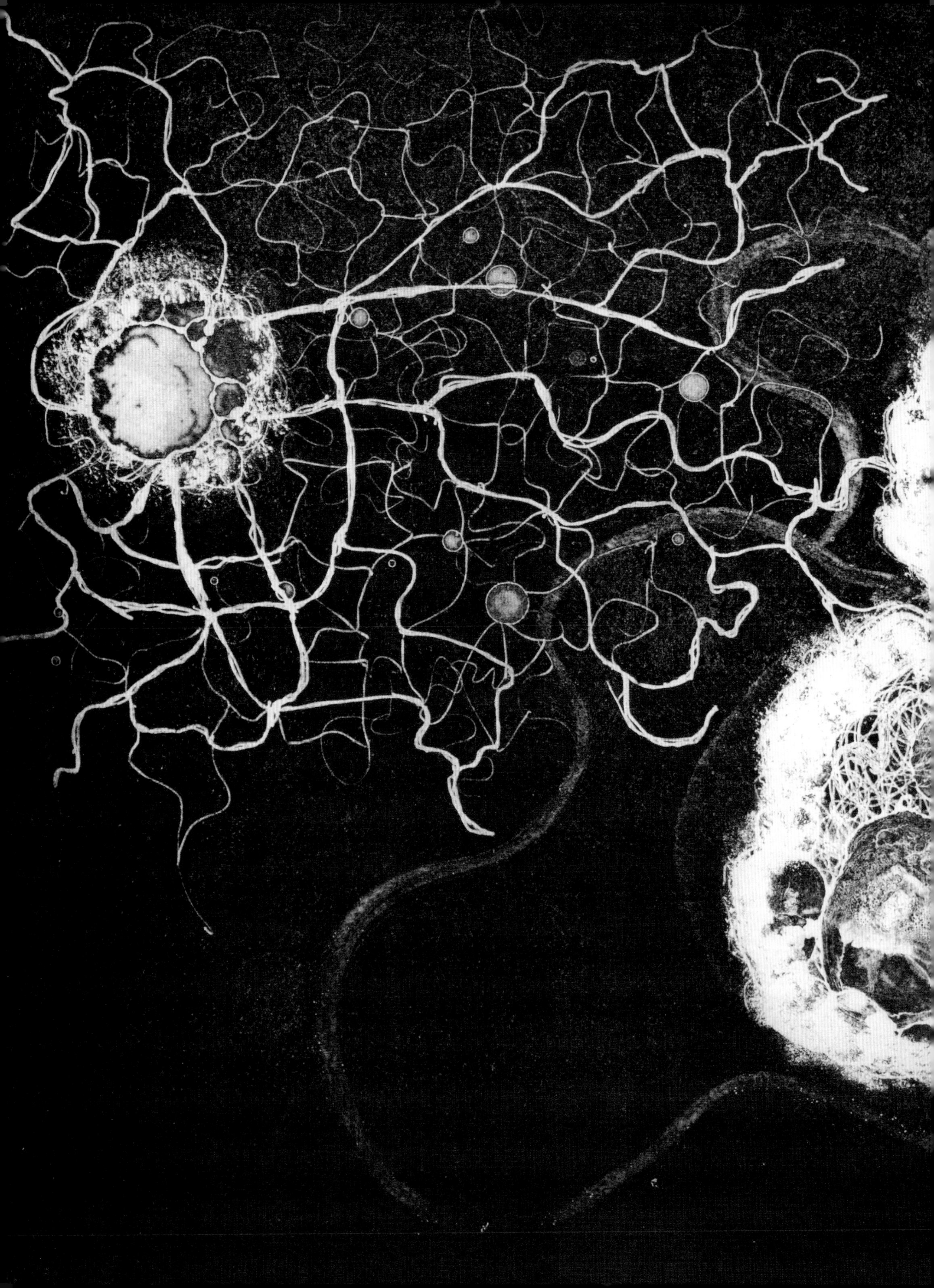

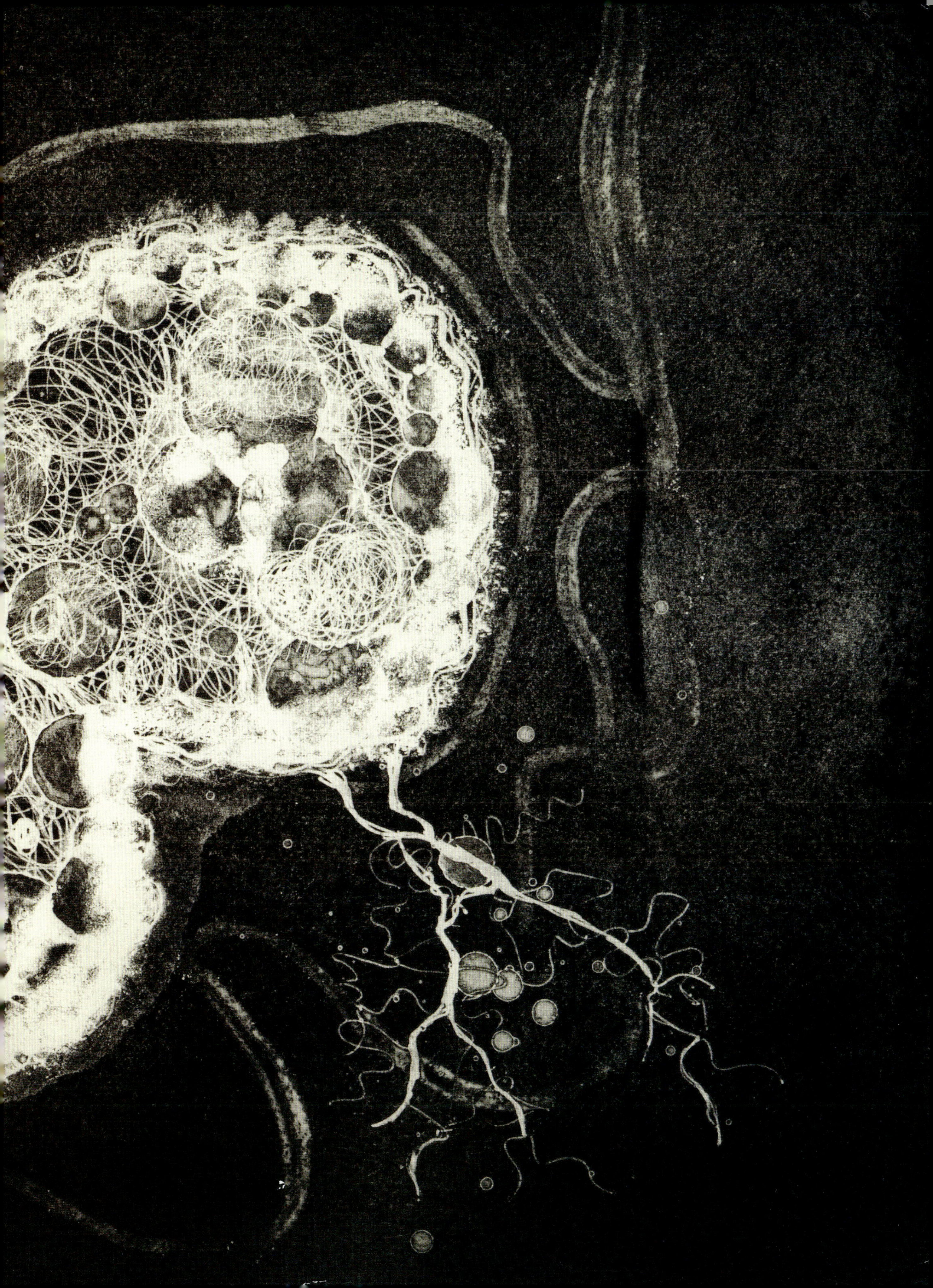

SCRIBING THE SOUL

Published in Great Britain in 2008
by Susan Aldworth
www.susanaldworth.com

ISBN 978-0-9558113-0-2

Designed and typeset by Paul Lussier Design
Printed in Great Britain by The Creative Group

ACKNOWLEDGEMENTS

I am grateful to the following:
The thirty patients who allowed me to observe their brain scans.
Dr Paul Butler for the opportunity to work in the neuroradiology unit at the Royal London Hospital, and Vital Arts for their support of my residency.
Nigel Oxley for his help in developing the etchings.
Jill Sheridan for project managing the tour and help in curating the exhibitions.
Michael Northeast and Barney Quinton for their work on my films.
Karen Taylor, Meli Hatzihrysidis and Sabine Unaman at Arts Council London, Esen Kaya at The Customs House, Sally Jane Norman, Professor Anya Hurlbert and Fiona Le Beau at Newcastle University, Dominic McDonald from Science Oxford, the staff at Peninsula Arts, and Cathy Lomax and Alex Michon from Transition Gallery, London.

Supported by
The National Lottery®
through Arts Council England

Arts Council England

IMAGES

front cover: **Location 23.2.05** acrylic ink and graphite 38 x 27 cms

page v: **Location 27.3.06** acrylic ink and graphite 38 x 27 cms

page vi: **Angiogram 6 2002** watercolour and graphite 17 x 13 cms

page viii: **Cogito Ergo Sum 3 2006** 20 giclée prints 175 x 140 cms

pages 38–9: **Birth of a Thought 2 2007** etching and aquatint 35 x 50 cms. Courtesy V&A

back cover: **Location 24.1.06** acrylic ink and graphite 38 x 27 cms